WAR
PROGRESS
AND THE
END OF HISTORY

WAR
PROGRESS
AND THE
END OF HISTORY

THREE CONVERSATIONS
Including a Short Story of the Anti-Christ

By
VLADIMIR SOLOVYOV

Introduction by
CZESLAW MILOSZ

Afterword by
STEPHAN A. HOELLER

Translated from the Russian by
ALEXANDER BAKSHY

Revised by
THOMAS R. BEYER JR.

Copyright © Lindisfarne Press 1990

All rights reserved. No part of this book, in part or in whole, may be reproduced, transmitted or utilized, in any form or by any means, electronic or mechanical, including photocopying, recording, or by any information storage and retrieval system, without permission in writing from the publisher, except for brief quotations in critical articles and reviews.

ISBN: 0-940262-35-5

Book design and production by Studio 31

CONTENTS

Introduction
by Czeslaw Milosz

Vladimir Solovyov is a great figure in the history of Russian religious thought elaborated by lay persons at the end of the nineteenth and the beginning of the twentieth centuries. His name is usually linked with those of thinkers belonging to the next generation: Nicholas Berdyayev (1874–1948), Lev Shestov (1866–1938), and Sergei Bulgakov (1871–1944) who became a priest.

Solovyov was born in 1853, into the family of Sergei Mikhailovich Solovyov, professor at the University of Moscow and author of the monumental *History of Russia from Most Ancient Times*. His mother came from the Ukraine and was related to the philosopher Hrihoriy Skovoroda. Thus, he belonged to the elite of the intelligentsia. Very gifted, well read from childhood, Solovyov distinguished himself at University and, in 1874, submitted his first important philosophical work as his master's thesis: *The Crisis of Western Philosophy: Against the Positivists*. As a teenager, he had gone through a religious crisis from which he emerged a convinced enemy of the atheism that resulted, according to him, from the scientific orientation of the West.

Prolific as a writer of philosophical books, Solovyov was also renowned as a poet. His poetry, in which he relates his mystical experiences, is read today as the testimony of a man who influenced the Russian symbolist movement. He is very much present in the history of Russian literature, thanks both to his ideas and his numerous polemics against his contemporaries, and because of his personal friendships — among others, his friendship as a young man with the aged Dostoevsky at the time the novelist was embarking on writing *The Brothers Karamazov*. There is a deep affinity between Dostoevsky's and Solovyov's beliefs and, according to literary legend, the figure of Alyosha Karamazov is modeled upon Solovyov.

Biographers of the poet-philosopher present him as an eccentric, a wanderer without a permanent address, and a nearly saintly altruist. In fact, in 1882, Solovyov abandoned his university career, dedicating himself to writing, living mostly on the landed estates of his friends, and giving away to the poor any money he earned, and not rarely also his clothes.

At the core of his philosophy, there is a vision of Sophia, Wisdom of God. According to legend, the most beautiful work of Byzantine art, the Church of Hagia Sophia (Holy Wisdom) in Byzantium (Istanbul), contributed to the conversion of the Kievan Rus' to Christianity in 988 A.D. At that time, Kiev's pagan prince hesitated between Judaism, Islam and the Christianity of Rome. The messengers he sent to Byzantium brought back the news that in Hagia Sophia "we felt as if in Heaven." Sophia (absent in Roman Catholicism) has been part of the tradition of the Eastern Church for many centuries, even appearing in some Russian icons as a fourth Person of the Holy Trinity. Markedly feminine, merging with the image of women often given that name, Sophia conveys the idea not only of wisdom but also of celestial beauty. No wonder that in Solovyov's vision she hardly differs from the Eternal Feminine. Solovyov, in fact, saw her three times as he describes in his poem "Three Meetings." The first vision he had as a youngster, the second as a young scholar in the reading room of the British Museum, and the third in Egypt, whither he had gone prompted by his inner voice promising a next meeting with her. Whatever we may think of these meetings, their literary presentation brings to mind the religious interpretation of marriage to be found in the Song of Songs: here the bridegroom and the bride are at the same time God in love with his creation or — the one does not exclude the other — with Israel, or with the human soul. In this way, the union of man and woman reflects the central arcanum of celestial sexuality.

This personification of Sophia suggests the strong current of Platonism in Eastern Christianity. In Solovyov's system, there is a certain hesitation with respect to Sophia's relation to the Deity: either she is a thought within God, or she is the soul (*anima*) of the world herself. Russian symbolist poets were especially sensitive to this aspect of Solovyov's teaching and, in their poetry, love for an unattainable Lady (unlike in the poetry of the Troubadours of Provence) often appears as acceding to a higher, ideal reality. This search may be found, above all, in the work of the eminent poet Alexander Blok (1880–1921). The Platonist aspect of Sophia was built up by Sergei Bulgakov — in his youth a Marxist, then a priest and theologian, professor at the Orthodox Institute in Paris — whose *oeuvre* develops a whole doctrine of Sophiology.

Among the numerous philosophical writings of Solovyov, his major works by their very titles indicate their contents: *Lectures on Godmanhood* (1877–81), *The Spiritual Foundations of Life* (1882–84), *The Great Controversy and Christian Policy* (1883), *The History and Future of Theocracy* (1885–87), *La Russie et L'Église Universelle* (1889), *The National Problem in Russia* (1883–91), *The Meaning of Love* (1892–94), and *The Justification of the Good* (1895).

In order to place Solovyov within the Russia of his time, it is necessary to stress his deep attachment to the Orthodox Church and his faith in the special Christian vocation of his country. This had strong messianic overtones. However he cannot be ranged with the Slavophiles with whom he engaged in public quarrels. Broadminded and devoid of chauvinism, Solovyov gradually moved away from praising the typically Russian unity of throne and altar to take an interest in Roman Catholicism, not only writing in an ecumenical spirit but also acting accordingly (receiving communion from a Catholic priest) — which gave rise to the unfounded rumors concerning his conversion. His concern with the unity of a Christianity divided into three great currents — Orthodoxy, Roman Catholicism, and Protestantism — is visible in *War, Progress, and the End of History: Three Conversations* in the prophecy of a great reconciliation.

Solovyov had an independent mind and was, in some respects, close to the opinions of the intelligentsia — though, after a short atheistic and socialistic period in his youth, he had no sympathy for revolutionaries. He supported the abolition of the death penalty and came to the defense of other nationalities oppressed by the Russian State. Yet, if for liberal opinion the name of Tolstoy epitomizes the ethical approach to society, while Dostoevsky puzzled, seduced, and terrified with his "reactionary" depth, Solovyov was definitely on Dostoevsky's side and an anti-Tolstoyan — though in his polemics he never attacked the novelist by name. *War, Progress, and the End of History: Three Conversations*, without using the name, is directed against Tolstoy (represented by one of the characters, the Prince) and his followers, as well as against a philosopher, Rousseau, who marked Tolstoy's thinking.

Paradoxically, Solovyov's religious philosophy, so rich and complex that it can hardly be touched upon in this introduction, is not lacking in traits which we would be inclined to call Tolstoyan, if only because of his belief in the victory of the good, his underestimation of evil, and a general optimistic tone. Read today, some of his treatises cannot but provoke the reflection that his hopes were not confirmed by the history of our century. As is the case of many nineteenth century meditations on society, we have often the impression of gentility and a lack of precision, perhaps the price to be paid for sharing the illusions his civilization nourished about itself. Solovyov assumed the continuous evolution of humanity toward a more and more humane life — an evolution that would lead finally to the Kingdom of God on earth. In this respect, his last book, *War, Progress, and the End of History: Three Conversations*, marks a turn in his thinking and, because it gives due attention to the power of evil, belongs already to our time — although it was written in 1899 (and finished in 1900, the year of Solovyov's death).

Thomas Mann considered Joseph Conrad's *Heart of Darkness* as the first literary work of the twentieth century, by virtue of both its title and its topic. Around 1900, dark forebodings began to visit literature, which proved to be more perspicacious than the rhetorics of journalism and public speeches. By criticizing the lofty talk of pacifists who announced the imminent arrival of universal peace, Solovyov joined those writers who voiced their misgivings about the possibility of a rosy future. Not unimportant is the fact that *War, Progress, and the End of History: Three Conversations* was written simultaneously with, if not in direct response to, an event widely publicized all over Europe at the time: the Hague Peace Conference of 1899, convoked at the initiative of Tsar Nicholas II of Russia.

It is difficult today to visualize cosmopolitan Europe prior to World War I. The Russian intelligentsia, an integral part of this cosmopolitan society, was justly famous for its fluency in foreign languages, its broadmindedness, and its deep interest in philosophy and poetry. *War, Progress, and the End of History: Three Conversations*, Solovyov's most literary work except for his poems, introduces characters who typify the attitudes of this intelligentsia, placing them within a definite geographic setting, the French Riviera, which was at the time visited by all the European social elite. The participants in the dialogue are the General, the Politician, the Lady, Mr. Z., and the Prince. Each one, in part, speaks for the author, especially Mr. Z., and all are very different from Russians as they have been visualized by the West since the Revolution of 1917.

The author's Preface is revealing. Whether true or invented, the story of the peasant worshipers of a hole in a beam is a perfect metaphor for the metaphysical void of a hollowed-out Christianity that leaves in its wake only a social, ethical message. Tolstoy, in his evangelical phase, rationalized the Gospels, and threw away the mystery of God incarnated. His own gospel of non-resistance to evil did not refer to the divine in Christ, who was for him (as for the earlier Saint-Simonians and the young Dostoevsky) only a bearer of socially progressive ideas. Solovyov, in his last work, tries to warn humanity of the consequences of such a purely horizontal religion reduced to ethics, without a vertical dimension. He foresees the temporary victory of such a false Christianity and the advent of the great Do-Gooder who is the Anti-Christ.

The parable of the Anti-Christ, presumably found in a manuscript of the monk Pansophius, is a powerful work. It makes use of an image, met with not rarely in Christian art — for instance in Italian woodcuts around 1500 or in the fresco by Luca Signorelli in Orvieto — in which the Anti-Christ combines demonic traits with traits of love and kindness. Solovyov endows his Anti-Christ with an almost archetypal vividness and creates a convincing biography of a man possessed by the Devil. Irresistibly, another parable comes to mind, that by Solovyov's friend Dostoevsky: "The Legend of the Grand Inquisitor," put into the mouth of Ivan in *The Brothers Karamazov*.

As a literary genre, Solovyov's tale may be compared with a variant of science fiction which, after the optimistic novels of Jules Verne, began around 1900 to depict the society of the future pessimistically — as in H. G. Wells' *The Time Machine*, and later in the works of Karel Capek, Eugen Zamyatin, Stacy Witkiewicz, Aldous Huxley, and George Orwell. *War, Progress, and the End of History: Three Conversa-*

tions is astonishingly prophetic and yet, in the way of all prophecy, particular parts of the whole are jumbled, perspectives are distorted, and the real and the improbable are mixed. We should therefore take this into account when we read of the strong state of Israel numbering thirty million inhabitants, or about the emergence of Islam as the main challenge to Europe. As to the invasion of Europe by a Japanese-Chinese army, in the last decade of the nineteenth century there was much talk about "The Yellow Peril" and this component of the parable should not surprise us much, especially if we take into account the obsessive fear of China quite common among Russians. In 1890, Solovyov himself published a treatise entitled *China and Europe*.

In *War, Progress, and the End of History: Three Conversations* Solovyov remained faithful to his belief in the final triumph of true Christianity, but he made a detour through the vast deserts of time under the control of the Prince of This World. Made cautious by historical tragedy which has caught in its grip innumerable inhabitants of our planet, we should read Solovyov's testament today as a letter addressed to *us*, one still of actuality.

August, 1990

Author's Preface

Is *evil* only a natural *defect*, an imperfection disappearing by itself with the growth of good, or is it a real *power*, *ruling* our world by means of temptations, so that to fight it success-fully assistance must be found in another sphere of being? This vital question can be fully examined and solved only in a complete system of metaphysics.

I began carrying out this task for those who are capable of contemplation, [1] but I soon felt how important the problem of evil is for everyone. Some two years ago a change in the tenor of my spiritual life (which there is no need to dwell upon now) created in me a strong and full desire to illumine in some clear and generally accessible way the main aspects of the problem of evil which, as I say, is of concern to all. For a long time, I was unable to find a suitable medium for carrying out my plan. Finally, in the spring of 1899, during my stay abroad, I spontaneously composed and wrote in a few days the first conversation on this subject; then, on returning to Russia, I wrote two others. In this way I discovered the literary form which this work assumes and which provided me with the simplest medium for the expression of the thoughts I wanted to communicate. This form of drawing-room conversation is a sufficient proof in itself that neither a scientifico-philosophical examination nor an orthodox sermon should be looked for in this work. My object was, rather, apologetic and polemic: I endeav-ored, as far as I could, to set out clearly and prominently the vital aspects of Christian truth, insofar as it is connected

---

[1] The introduction to this work was published by me in the first chapters of my *Theoretical Philosophy* — Author.

15

with the question of evil, and to disperse the fog in which everybody seems to have been trying lately to enwrap it.

Many years ago I happened to read about a new religion that was founded in the eastern provinces of Russia. The religion, the followers of which called themselves "Hole Drillers," or "Hole Worshipers," was very simple; a middle-sized hole was drilled in a wall in some dark corner of a house, and individuals put their mouths to it and repeated earnestly: " My house, my hole, save me!" Never before, I believe, has the object of worship been reduced to such a degree of simplicity. It must be admitted, however, that, though the worship of an ordinary peasant's house and of a simple hole made by human hands in its wall was a palpable error, it was a truthful error; those people were absolutely mad, but they did not deceive anybody; the house they worshiped they called a *house*, and the hole drilled in the wall they reasonably termed merely a *hole*.

But the religion of the hole worshipers soon underwent a process of "evolution" and was subjected to "transformation." It still retained in its new form its former weakness of religious thought and its narrow character of philosophic interests, its former *terre-à-terre* realism, but it completely lost its past truthfulness. The "house" now was called "the Kingdom of God *on Earth*," and the "hole" received the name of "the new Gospel," while the distinction between the sham gospel and the true one (and this is the most distressing fact about it), a distinction which is exactly similar to that existing between a hole drilled in a beam and the complete living tree — this essential distinction was either neglected or confused by the new evangelists.

Of course, I do not draw a direct historical or "genetic" connection between the original sect of hole worshipers and the teaching of the sham Kingdom of God and the sham Gospel. Neither is it important for my objective, which is only to show clearly the essential identity of the two "teachings" with the above moral distinction. The identity here lies in the purely negative and void character of both "doctrines". It is true that the "educated" hole worshipers do not call themselves by this name but go under the name of Christians, and that their teaching is also passed off as the Gospel. But Christianity without Christ and the Gospel, i.e., the *good news*, without the only *good* worth announcing — without the real resurrection to the fullness of blessed life — these are as much a *hollow space* as is the ordinary hole drilled in a peasant's house.

There would not be any need to speak about this at all were it not for the fact that over the rationalist hole the Christian flag is flown, tempting and confusing many of the "little ones." When the people who believe and cautiously declare that Christ has become *obsolete* and has been *superseded*, or that he never existed at all, and that his life is a myth invented by Paul, at the same time persistently call themselves "true Christians" and screen their teaching of hollow space by distorted quotations from the Gospel, it is well-nigh time to put aside our indifference to and our condescending contempt for their opinions. The moral atmosphere is contaminated with systematic falsehoods, so the public conscience loudly demands that the evil work should be branded by its real name. The true object of polemics in this case would be *not the confuting of sham religion but the showing up of the actual fraud.*

This fraud has no excuse. Between me (the author of three books banned by ecclesiastic censorship) on the one side and these publishers of numerous foreign books, pamphlets, and leaflets on the other side, the question of external obstacles to an unreserved frankness in these matters does not seriously arise. The restraints of religious freedom existing in our country cause the greatest pain to my heart, for I see and feel to what a great extent these restrictions bring harm to and impose burdens not only on those whom they directly affect, but mainly on the cause of Christianity in Russia, consequently on the Russian nation, and ultimately on the Russian State.

No external situation can prevent a man who is honestly convinced in his opinions from stating them fully. If it is impossible to do so at home, one can do it abroad; and none have availed themselves of this opportunity to a greater extent than the teachers of the sham Gospel have done when the matters concerned have been the *practical* questions of politics and religion. As regards the main, the *essential* question, there is no need even to go abroad in order to refrain from insincerity and artifice: the Russian censorship never demands that we pronounce opinions we do not hold, that we simulate a faith in things we do not believe in, or that we love and revere what we despise and hate. To maintain an honest attitude toward the known historical Person and His Work, the preachers of hollowness had only one thing to do in Russia: they should merely have *ignored* him. But here is the strange fact. In this matter, these preachers refuse to avail themselves either of the freedom of silence which they enjoy at home or of the freedom of speech which they enjoy abroad. Both here and there they prefer to show their allegiance to the Gospel of Christ; both here and there they decline to reveal honestly their real attitude to the Founder of Christianity either by a resolute word or by an eloquent silence — they do not show that He is entirely alien to them, is for no object required and is only a hindrance in their way.

From their point of view, the things they preach are *of themselves* clear, desirable, and salutary for all. Their "truth" is self-supporting and, if a certain historical person — Jesus — happens to agree with it, so much the better for him, though this fact does not endow him with any special authority in their eyes, particularly when it is remembered that this person has said and done many things which for these people are nothing but a "temptation" and "madness."

Even supposing that these moralists, in their very human weakness, feel an irresistible desire to sustain their beliefs as well as their own "reason" by some historical authority, why, I ask, do they not look in history for *another* who shall be a more suitable representative? For a long time, there has been one waiting for such recognition — the founder of the widely popular religion of Buddhism. Buddha really did preach what they required — nonresistance, impossibility, inactivity, sobriety, etc. — and succeeded even *without martyrdom* "in making a brilliant career"[2] for his religion. The sacred books of the Buddhists do really proclaim *hollowness*; and, to make them fully agree with the new teaching of the same matter, they would require only a little simplification in detail. The Scriptures of the Jews and the Christians, on the other hand, are permeated throughout by a positive spiritual message that denies both ancient and modern emptiness, so that, to be able to fasten the teaching of Buddhism to any of the statements taken from the Gospel or the Prophets, it is necessary, by hook or by crook, to tear away such a statement from its natural connection with the whole of the book and the context. Whereas, on the other hand, the Buddhist "sutras" supply whole masses of suitable parables and legends, and there is nothing in those books inimical in spirit to the new teaching.

By substituting the hermit of the Sacciah tribe for the "rabbi from Galilee," the sham Christians would have lost nothing of importance, but would win something very valuable indeed, at least in my eyes. They would win the possibility of thinking, even while erring, honestly and, to an extent, consistently. But they do not want this.

The hollowness of the teaching of the new "religion" and its logical contradictions are too apparent; and, in this

[2] Not my expression — Author.

matter, I have been satisfied to give (in the Third Conversation) only a brief, though complete, statement of their
pronouncements, obviously contradictory in themselves
and hardly capable of tempting anybody outside the hopeless class of people typified by my Prince. Should I succeed
in opening anybody's eyes to the other side of the question
and making any deceived but living soul feel all the moral
falsity of this death-spreading teaching taken in all its
entirety, the polemical object of this book would be fully
achieved.

I am firmly convinced, however, that the exposure of an
untruth made without reservation, should it even fail to
produce any beneficent effect, still remains, apart from the
fulfillment of duty it involves for its author, a measure of
spiritual sanitation in the life of society and brings useful
results in both the present and the future.

Bound up with the polemical object of these dialogues is
a positive aim: to present the question of the struggle
against evil and of the meaning of history from three
different standpoints. One of these is based on a religious
conception of the everyday life, which is characteristic of
past times, and is given much prominence in the First
Conversation in the speeches of *the General*. A second
standpoint, representing the ideas of culture and progress
prevailing in our time, is expressed and defended by *the
Politician*, particularly in the Second Conversation. The
third standpoint, which is absolutely religious and which
will yet show its decisive value in the future, is indicated in
the Third Conversation in the speeches of *Mr. Z.* and in the
story by Father Pansophius. Personally, I unreservedly
accept the last point of view. But I fully recognize the
relative truth contained in the two others and, for this
reason, could with equal fairness express the opposing
arguments and statements of *the Politician* and *the General*.
The higher absolute truth does not exclude or deny
the preliminary conditions of its realization, but justifies,

appreciates, and sanctifies them. If from a certain point of view the world's history is God's judgment of the world — *die Weltgeschichte ist das Weltgericht* — this judgment involves a long and complicated lawsuit or litigation between the good and the evil historical forces, and this suit, to come to a final solution, must involve both a determined struggle for existence between those forces, and their greater inner, therefore peaceful, development in the common forms of culture. For this reason, the General and the Politician are both right in the light of a higher truth, and I could with complete sincerity place myself in the position of either one or the other. It is only the power of evil itself that is absolutely wrong, but not such means of fighting as the sword of the soldier or the pen of the diplomat afford. These *tools* must be appraised at their actual usefulness in the given circumstances, and that must be considered the better of the two whose use is more effective in upholding the cause of good. St. Alexis the metropolitan, when peacefully pleading for the Russian princes at the Tartar Horde, and St. Sergius, when blessing the arms of Dmitrius of the Don against the same Horde, equally served both one and the same cause of good, thereby demonstrating that "good" finds its expression in many various forms and fashions.

These conversations about evil and about the militant and the peaceful methods of combating it had to be concluded with a definite statement of the last, the extremist manifestation of evil in history, the picture of its short-lived triumph and its final destruction. At first I treated this subject in the form of a dialogue, as I had treated the other parts, and with a similar sprinkling of jocularity. But friendly criticisms convinced me that this method of exposition was doubly unsuitable: first, because the interruptions and interpolations required by the form of dialogue tended to weaken the interest in the story; and, second, because the colloquial and particularly the jocular character of conversation did not accord with the subject's religious importance. I recognized the justice of these criticisms and, accordingly, altered the form of the Third Conversation, introducing in it the reading from a manuscript left by a monk after his death and containing an independent "Short Story of the Anti-Christ."

This story, which earlier formed the subject of a public lecture, created a good deal of bewilderment and confused comment in society and in the press, the main reason for which appears to be very simple: the prevailing insufficient knowledge of the references to the Anti-Christ contained in the Scriptures and in Church tradition. These give indications of all his main features, such as his inner significance as a religious impostor who obtains the title of the Son of God by "stealing" it and not by spiritual self-sacrifice; his connection with a false prophet or wizard who seduces people by means of real and false miracles; the obscure and peculiarly sinful origin of the Anti-Christ himself who secures his external position as monarch of the world by the help of evil powers; and the general development and the end of his activity. Other particulars, characteristic of the Anti-Christ and his false prophet, may also be found in the same sources. We have there, for instance, "the bringing down of fire from Heaven," the murdering of the two witnesses of Christ, and exposure of their bodies in the streets of Jerusalem. All of this is found in the Scriptures and ancient tradition. To connect the events with each other and to make the story more expressive, several details had to be introduced, partly based on historical conjectures and partly created by imagination. On the imaginative details, such as the semi-psychic, semi-conjuring tricks of the great magician with subterranean voices, fireworks, and so forth, I placed, it hardly needs saying, very little importance, and I think I was justified in expecting a similar attitude on the part of my "critics." As regards the other and extremely essential point — the characteristics of the three impersonated confessions in the ecumenical council

— this could be noticed and fully appreciated only by those of my critics who were acquainted with the history and life of the churches.

The character of the false prophet and his mission to mystify people for the benefit of Anti-Christ (as clearly indicated in Revelation) made it necessary for me to attribute to him different prodigies of the kind peculiar to magicians and conjurers. It is known for a certainty, *dass sein Hauptwerk ein Feuerwerk sein wird*: "and he doeth great wonders, so that he maketh *fire* come down from heaven on the earth in the sight of men." (Revelation, xiii. 13.) At present we cannot, of course, know the magic and mechanical technique of these prodigies, but we may be sure that in two or three centuries our understanding will advance very far from what it is now, and what will be made possible by such progress for a magician like ours is not for me to say. I have admitted into my story definite features and details only as concrete illustrations of its essential and well-established relations, so that these would not be left mere bare outlines.

The essentials and the details should also be clearly distinguished in all that I say about Pan-Mongolism and the Asiatic invasion of Europe. But, of course, the main fact itself has not, in this case, the absolute certainty which characterizes the future coming and the fate of the Anti-Christ and his false prophet. Nothing has been taken directly from the Scriptures in describing the development of the Mongol-European relations, though a great deal of it can be based on Scriptural statements. Taken in general, the history indicated presents a series of conjectures of the probable based on the actual facts. Personally, I believe this probability to be very near the certainty, and my projection is shared by many much more important personages. For the sake of the coherency of the story, several details had to be introduced into these considerations of the coming Mongolian menace, details for which I, of course, cannot vouch and which, on the whole, I tried not to abuse. The thing of much greater importance to me was to make the picture of the coming terrific conflict of the two worlds as realistic as possible, and to show thereby the pressing necessity of peace and true friendship among all the nations of Europe.

If the cessation of war *in general* seems to me impossible before the final catastrophe is over, I do firmly believe that the closest friendship and peaceful cooperation of all the *Christian* nations and states is not only a possible but a necessary and morally imperative way to prevent the salvation of the Christian world from being swallowed up by lower elements.

So as not to make the story too long and too complicated, I had to leave out another conjecture of mine which deserves a few words of explanation. It seems to me that the coming success of Pan-Mongolism will be greatly facilitated by the stubborn and exhausted struggle which some of the European countries will have to wage against the awakened Islam in Western Asia and in North and Central Africa. A greater part than it is generally believed will be played in that awakening by the secret and incessant activity of the religious and political brotherhood of "Senussi" which has, for the movements of modern Islam, the same guiding importance as in the movements of the Buddhist world belongs to the Tibetan brotherhood of "Kelani" in Lhasa, with all its Indian, Chinese, and Japanese ramifications. I am far from being absolutely hostile to Buddhism, neither am I particularly so to Islam. But a willful blindness to the existing and coming state of things is too readily indulged in by many people today, and I might perhaps have chosen for myself a more profitable occupation.

The historical forces reigning over the masses of humanity will yet have to come to blows and become intermingled with each other before the new head grows on the self-lacerating body of the beast: the world-unifying power of the Anti-Christ, who "will speak loud and high-sounding words," and will cast a glittering veil of good and truth over the mystery of utter lawlessness in the time of its final revelation, so that even the chosen, in the words of the Scriptures, will be reduced to the great betrayal. To show beforehand this deceptive visor, under which is concealed the evil abyss, was my highest aim in writing this book.

Concluding, I must express my sincere gratitude to Mr. A. P. Salomon, who corrected and supplemented my topographical data of modern Jerusalem; to Mr. N. A. Veliaminov, who communicated to me the story of the Bashi-Bazouk "kitchen," which he personally witnessed in 1877; and to Mr. M. Bibikov, who carefully examined the General's narrative in the First Conversation and pointed out some errors from the military standpoint which have now been amended.

Even in this amended form, however, I still feel the numerous defects of the work. But not less felt is also the distant image of pale death, which quietly advises me not to put off the publication of this book to an indefinite and little secure date. Shall I be given time for new works, I shall be given it for improving the old ones as well. If not, the statement of the coming historical issue of the moral struggle has been made by me in sufficiently clear, though brief, outlines, and I publish this little work with the grateful feeling of a fulfilled moral duty.

Vladimir Solovyov
Easter, 1900

Note

This preface was originally published in the newspaper *Russia*, under the title "On the False Good." When preparing "The First Conversation" for publication as a separate volume, V. Solovyov made numerous textual corrections. In a fateful manner, however, one of these corrections has proved unnecessary. On the advice of his friends he struck out the words which seemed to bear too personal a character, i.e., "but not less felt is also the distant image of pale death, which quietly advises me not to put off the publication. . . ." These words, which were only too soon justified, should remain in the amended text as it stands now.

M. Solovyov
(Editor of the Russian edition).

Vladimir Solovyov died on July 31, 1900.

[TRB]

WAR
PROGRESS
AND THE
END OF HISTORY

THE SCENE

In the garden of one of the villas that nestle together under the foothills of the Alps and gaze into the azure depths of the Mediterranean, five Russians happened to meet together this spring: an old GENERAL; a statesman enjoying a hard-earned rest from the whirl and turmoil of politics whom I shall henceforth call the POLITICIAN; a young PRINCE whose strong democratic views and thirst for reform had led him to publish a large number of more or less valuable pamphlets on moral and social progress; a middle-aged LADY, very inquisitive and greatly interested in humanity at large; and another gentleman, of somewhat uncertain age and social position, whom we shall call MR. Z.

I myself was a silent listener at the frequent conversations which took place among them. Certain of these conversations appeared to me to be particularly interesting; I therefore took care to write them down while they were still fresh in my mind. The first conversation was started in my absence and was provoked by some newspaper article or pamphlet on the literary campaign against war and military service, a campaign originated by Count Tolstoy and now being carried on by Baroness Zutner and Mr. Stead. The POLITICAN, questioned by the LADY as to his opinion of this peace movement, characterized it as being well-intentioned and useful. This statement immediately called forth angry remarks from the GENERAL, who began to sneer at these three writers calling them, ironically, the true pillars of statesmanlike wisdom, guiding stars on the political horizon, and even dubbing them the three "whales" of Russia. [1] To this latter remark, the POLITICIAN rejoined: "Well, there may be other *fish*." This, for some reason, greatly delighted MR. Z. who, according to his own account, subsequently forced both opponents to agree to regard the whale as a fish and to assent to his definition of a fish as an animal belonging partly to the Admiralty and partly to the Department of Waterways — a story that was not, I believe, a pure invention of MR. Z. Be that as it may, I was unable to reconstruct the real beginning of the conversation and therefore, being afraid to compose it out of my own head after the model of Plato and his imitators, I begin my account with the words uttered by the GENERAL, just as I joined the company.

---

[1] According to Russian folklore the earth rests on three whales — Translator.

CHAPTER ONE

THE FIRST CONVERSATION
Audiatur et prima *pars*

GENERAL (*excited; speaks incessantly, getting up and sitting down with many rapid gestures*) – Oh, no! How is that? Oh, no! No! Answer me this one question: Does such a thing as a *Christ-loving* and *glorious Russian Army* truly exist at this moment? Yes or no?

POLITICIAN (*lounging comfortably in an easy chair, and speaking in a tone suggestive of a compound of Epicurus, a Prussian colonel, and Voltaire*) – Does a Russian Army exist? Obviously it does. Why, you surely haven't heard that it had been abolished?

GENERAL – How terribly ingenuous you are to be sure! You understand perfectly well that that is not what I mean. I ask you this: Am I right in regarding our present army as a glorious band of Christ-loving warriors, or am I to suppose that one ought to call it something else?

POLITICIAN – I see! That's what bothers you, is it? Well, you have brought your question to the wrong shop. You should inquire at the Department of Heraldry. They are the recognized experts in titles, I believe.

MR. Z. (*speaking as if he had an idea at the back of his mind*) – And the Department of Heraldry will probably tell the General that the law places no restriction on the use of old titles. Did not the last Prince Lusignan hold the title of King of Cyprus, although he not only had no jurisdiction in Cyprus, but could not even drink Cyprian wine owing to his weak stomach and empty purse? Why, then, shouldn't

the modern army be entitled a Christ-loving band of
warriors?

GENERAL – Entitled! Then we may call black and white
titles? So are sweet and bitter and so are hero and scoundrel.

MR. Z. – But I am not stating my own opinion. I merely
put forward what appears to be held by people who should
know!

LADY (*to the Politician*) – Why do you argue about mere
forms of expression? I am sure the General meant to say
something with his "Christ-loving band of warriors."

GENERAL – I thank you, madam. What I wished, and
what I still wish to say is this: From earliest times until but
yesterday, every warrior, whether a private or a field
marshal, knew and felt that he served in a good and
important cause. He believed not only that he fulfilled
duties every bit as necessary as sanitation or washing for
instance, but also that he was part of a service which was
good, honorable, and noble in the highest sense of the
word, and to which the greatest and best men that ever
lived — heroes and leaders of nations — have given their
lives. This cause of ours has always been sanctified and
exalted by the Church and glorified by the praise of the
nation. And yet, behold! One fine morning we are told that
we must forget all this and that we soldiers must hold
ourselves and our place in the world to be the very
opposite. The cause which we have served, and always
have been proud of serving, is suddenly declared to be a
thing of evil and a menace to the country. Warfare, it
appears, is against God's express commandments, is entirely opposed to human sentiments, and inevitably brings
about the most dreadful evil and dire misfortune. All
nations, we are told, must combine against it and make its
final destruction only a question of time.

PRINCE – Do you mean to tell us that you have never

before heard opinions which utterly condemn war and military service as relics of ancient barbarism?

GENERAL – Who has not? Of course I have heard them, and have read them, too, in more languages than one! But all such puny voices — you must pardon my frankness — seem to me by no means the thunderclaps that you consider them. And, yet, today matters are different; one must listen to these opinions, expressed as they are on all sides. What on earth are we to do? Am I — and for that matter, every other soldier — to regard myself as an honorable man or as an inhuman monster? Am I to respect myself as a willing servant in a noble cause, or am I to view my occupation with abhorrence, to repent of my misdeeds in sackcloth and ashes, and to beg for pardon on my knees for the sins of my profession from every civilian?

POLITICIAN – What a fantastic way of stating the question! As if anyone were asking you anything extraordinary. The new demands are addressed, not to you, but to diplomats and other "civilians" who care precious little whether soldiers are vicious or Christ-loving. As far as you yourself are concerned, there is only one demand placed upon you: to carry out unquestioningly the orders of the authorities.

GENERAL – Well, well! As you take no interest in military matters, it is only natural that your idea of them should be "fantastic", to use your own expression. You are obviously unaware that, in certain cases, the order of the authorities has no other meaning than that you must neither wait nor ask for their orders.

POLITICIAN – For instance?

GENERAL – For instance, just imagine that by the will of the powers that be, I am placed in command of a whole military district. From this very fact, it follows that I am commanded to govern and control in every way the troops placed in my charge. I am to develop and strengthen in them a definite point of view — to act in some definite way on their will — to influence their feelings; in a word, to educate them, so to speak, up to the purpose of their being. Very well then. For this purpose I am empowered, among other things, to issue to the troops of my district general orders in my name and entirely on my personal responsibility. Well, if I should apply to my superior officers, asking them to dictate to me my orders, or merely to instruct me in what form they should be drawn up, don't you think I should, in return, be dubbed "an old fool?" And that, if it happened again, I should be summarily dismissed? This means that I must adopt toward my troops a consistent policy, some definite spirit which, it is supposed, has been previously and once and for all approved and confirmed by the higher command, so that even to inquire about it would be to show either stupidity or impertinence. At present, however, this "definite spirit" — which, as a matter of fact, has been one and the same from the times of Sargon and Assurbanipal to those of William II — suddenly proves to be under suspicion. Until yesterday, I knew that I had to develop and strengthen in my troops not a new but this same old *fighting* spirit, the willingness of each individual soldier to conquer the enemy or to go to his death. And, for this, it is absolutely necessary to possess an unshaken faith in war as a holy cause. But now this faith is being deprived of its spiritual basis, military work is losing what the learned call "its moral and religious sanction."

POLITICIAN – How frightfully exaggerated all this is! In reality there is no such radical change of views. On the one hand, everyone has always recognized that war is evil and that the less there is of it the better. On the other hand, all serious people today realize that war is the kind of evil that it is impossible at present to eradicate completely. Consequently, the question is not whether war can be abolished but whether it can be gradually, even if very slowly, reduced to the narrowest limits. The principal attitude toward war remains what it has always been: war is an unavoidable evil, a misfortune, tolerable only in extreme cases.

GENERAL – And nothing else?

POLITICIAN – Nothing else.

GENERAL (*springing up from his seat*) – Have you ever had occasion to refer to the Book of Saints?

POLITICIAN – You mean in the calendar? Oh yes, I have sometimes to run through a long list of the names of patron saints in order to find the name-days of certain friends and relatives.

GENERAL – Did you notice what saints are mentioned there?

POLITICIAN – There are different kinds of saints.

GENERAL – But what are their callings?

POLITICIAN – Their callings are as different as their names, I believe.

GENERAL – That's just where you are wrong. Their callings are not different.

POLITICIAN – What? Surely *all* the saints are not military men?

GENERAL – Not all, but half of them.

POLITICIAN – Exaggeration again!

GENERAL – We are not taking a census for statistical purposes here. What I maintain is that all the saints of our Russian church belong only to two classes: they are either monks of various orders, or princes — men who, from what we know of past history, must have been military men. And we have no other saints, I mean those of the male sex. Monk or warrior, that is all.

LADY – You are forgetting "God's fools" aren't you?

GENERAL – Not at all! But "God's fools" are a kind of irregular monks, aren't they? What Cossacks are to the army, "God's fools" are to the monkhood. This being so, if you now find for me among the Russian saints a single clergyman, or tradesman, or deacon, or clerk, or commoner, or peasant — in a word, a person of any profession other than that of monk and soldier — then you may take the whole of any winnings I may bring home from Monte Carlo next Sunday.

POLITICIAN – Thank you very much. Keep your treasures and your half of the Book of Saints — the whole of it, if you like. But do please explain what it is that you are trying to prove by this discovery of yours. Is it only that nobody but a monk or a soldier can set us a true example of moral life?

GENERAL – That is hardly the point. I myself have known many highly virtuous people among the clergy, bankers, the official classes, and the peasants. The most virtuous person I can recollect was the old nurse of one of my friends. But we are not talking about this. I mentioned the saints only to point out that it could hardly have been possible for so many soldiers to become saints, side by side with monks and in preference to members of every other peaceful and civic profession, if the military occupations were always regarded as a necessary evil — as something like the liquor traffic, or even worse. It is clear that the Christian nations, at whose behest the Books of Saints were actually compiled (and this is so not only with the Russians but with other nations as well), not only respected the military calling, but they *particularly* respected it; and, of all the lay professions, only the military was held fit to contribute members to the saintship. It is this view that seems incompatible with the modern campaign against war.

POLITICIAN – But I did not say that there is *no* change whatever. Some desirable change is undoubtedly taking place. It is true that the halo which crowned warriors and their wars in the eyes of the masses is fast disappearing. Matters have been tending this way for a long time now. Besides, whose interests does this actually affect? Only those of the clergy, I should say, as the manufacture of *auréoles* belongs exclusively to its department. Some difficulties will need to be cleared up here, of course. And what cannot be suppressed will be interpreted symbolically, while the rest will wisely be kept quiet or relegated to oblivion.

PRINCE – These modifications are already being made. In connection with my publications I have to watch our ecclesiastical literature, and in two papers I had the pleasure of reading that Christianity absolutely condemns war.

GENERAL – Is that really so?

PRINCE – I myself could scarcely believe my own eyes. But I can show it to you.

POLITICIAN (*to the General*) – You see! Why, though, should you be worried about it? Aren't you warriors men of deeds and not of windy words? Is all this merely professional selfishness and ambition on your part? If it is, it is certainly bad of you. But I repeat: in practice, everything remains for you as before. Let it be true that the system of militarism, which for thirty years has been an insupportable burden to everyone, is now bound to disappear. Of course, an army of some size must still remain. And insofar as we admit that it is necessary, just so far will the same fighting qualities as before be demanded of it.

GENERAL – That's it. You are all great masters at demanding milk of a dead bull! But who is to give you the required fighting qualities, when the first fighting quality (without which all others are of little use) is a cheerful and confident spirit, itself the outcome of faith in the sacredness of the cause to which one has devoted oneself? How can this be achieved, when war is considered a crime and a villainy, and is tolerated only in certain extreme cases as an unfortunate necessity?

POLITICIAN – Nobody expects this to be believed by the military. If they choose to consider themselves as the best people in the world, who cares? It's nobody's business but their own. It was explained to you before, was it not, that Prince Lusignan is allowed to style himself the King of

Cyprus, provided he does not ask us to give him money for Cyprian wine. So if you do not raid our pockets more than is necessary, you may regard yourselves the salt of the earth and the flower of humanity — nobody will stop you.

General – You say, "regard yourselves"! But, surely, we are not talking on the moon. Are you going to keep soldiers in a Toricellian vacuum, so that no foreign influences can reach them? And this in the days of universal military service, a short period of training, and cheap newspapers! No, the matter is only too clear. Once military service is compulsory for each and everyone, and once this new negative attitude toward the military profession becomes universally adopted throughout the whole of society, from such eminent representatives of the State as yourself, for example, to the lowest, this view must needs be assimilated by the soldiers themselves. If all, from the higher command downward, begin to regard military service as an evil, inevitable only for *the present*, then, in the first place, individuals will never of their own accord choose the military calling for their life's work — with the exception perhaps of the dregs of society who can find no other career open to them — and secondly, all those who will be compelled to bear limited military service will do so with feelings similar to those with which criminals, chained to wheelbarrows, carry their fetters. Talk of fighting qualities and fighting spirit under such conditions! What drivel!

Mr. Z. – I have always believed that, after the introduction of universal military service, the abolition of armies, and eventually of individual States, is only a question of time, a time not far removed from the present moment, considering the accelerated progress of events.

General – Perhaps you are right.

Prince – I think that you are *most certainly* right, though the idea has never occurred to my mind in this guise. But it is splendid! Only think: militarism creates, as its most extreme expression, the system of universal military service, and then, owing to this very fact, not only modern militarism, but the very foundations of the military system as such, become utterly destroyed. Isn't it wonderful!

LADY – Look! Even the Prince's face has brightened up. This is a pleasant change. The Prince has up to now been wearing a gloomy countenance, ill suited to his profession of "true Christian."

PRINCE – One sees so many sad things around. There is but one joy left: the thought that reason will inevitably triumph, despite all obstacles.

MR. Z. – There can be no doubt that militarism in Western Europe and Russia is feeding upon itself. But as to the joys and triumphs which are to proceed from this fact — those remain to be seen.

PRINCE – What? Do you doubt that war and militarism are *absolute* and *utter* evils, of which humanity must rid itself *at any cost* and *immediately*? Do you doubt that the complete and immediate suppression of this barbarism would result *in any case* in a triumph for reason and good?

MR. Z. – I am positively certain of quite *the opposite*.

PRINCE – That is, of what?

MR. Z. – Of the fact that war is *not* an absolute evil, and that peace is not an absolute good, or, putting it in a simpler way, that it is possible to have (as we do have sometimes) such a thing as *a good war*, and that it is also possible to have (as we do have sometimes) *an evil peace*.

PRINCE – Now I see the difference between your view and that held by the General: he believes, doesn't he, that war is always a good thing, and that peace is always a bad thing?

GENERAL – By no means! I understand perfectly well that sometimes war can be a very bad thing, as, for instance, was the case when we were beaten at Narva or at Austerlitz. And peace can also be a splendid thing, as, for example, the peace concluded at Nystad or at Kuchuk-Kainardji. [2]

LADY – Is this a variant of the famous saying of the Kaffir or Hottentot who told the missionary that he understood very well the difference between what is good and what is evil: — "Good is when I carry away somebody else's wives and cows, and evil is when mine are carried away from me"?

GENERAL – Don't you see that I was trying to say something witty? The humor of your African's remark may have been unintended; the humor of my remark was intentional. But now let us hear how clever people discuss the question of war from the standpoint of morals.

POLITICIAN – I would only wish that our "clever people" do not land us in scholasticism and metaphysics when discussing so perfectly clear and historically limited a problem.

PRINCE – Clear from what point of view?

POLITICIAN – My point of view is an ordinary one, a European one, one that is being gradually assimilated by cultured people, even in other parts of the world.

PRINCE – And its essence is, of course, that everything is considered relatively and that no absolute difference is admitted between "must" and "must not," between good and evil. Isn't this so?

MR. Z. – Pardon me. But this argument seems to me rather useless in relation to the problem we are discussing. To take myself, for instance, I fully recognize the absolute opposition between moral good and evil. At the same time, it is perfectly clear to me that war and peace do not come

[2] The Treaty of Nystad (1721) between Russia and Sweden concluded the Great Northern War and the period of Sweden's military greatness; the Treaty of Kuchuk-Kainarji (1774) followed Turkey's war with Russia — Editor.

within the scope of the argument; it is quite impossible to paint war solid black and peace all pure white.

PRINCE – But this involves an internal contradiction. If a thing that is evil in itself — for instance, murder — can be good in certain cases, as when you are pleased to call it war, what becomes then of the absolute difference between evil and good?

MR. Z. – How simple it is for you! "Every kind of murder is absolute evil; war is murder; it follows then that war is absolute evil." The syllogism is first rate! The only thing you lose sight of is that both your premises, the major and the minor, have first to be proved and that, consequently, your conclusion so far rests on air.

POLITICIAN – Didn't I tell you we would land in scholasticism?

LADY – What are they talking about?

POLITICIAN – Oh, some sort of major and minor premises.

MR. Z. – Pardon me. We are just now getting down to business. (*To the Prince*) You do maintain at any rate, don't you, that killing, taking somebody's life, is absolute evil?

PRINCE – Undoubtedly.

MR. Z. – But to be killed — is this absolute evil or not?

PRINCE – From the Hottentot standpoint, of course it is. But we have been discussing moral evil, and this can exist only in the actions of an intelligent being in control of itself, not in what happens to that being independently of its will. It follows that to be killed is the same as to die from cholera or influenza. Not only is it not absolute evil, it is not evil at all. Socrates and the Stoics have already taught us this.

MR. Z. – Well, I cannot answer for people so ancient as those. As to your moral appreciation of murder, this seems to limp somewhat. According to you, it follows that absolute evil consists in causing a person something that is not evil at all. Think what you like, but there is something lame here. However, we will leave this lameness alone lest we really land in scholasticism. To sum up, in killing the evil is not in the physical fact of a life being taken but in the moral cause of this fact, namely, in the evil will of the one who kills. Do you agree?

PRINCE – It is so, of course. For without this evil will there is no murder but only misfortune or inadvertence.

MR. Z. – Clearly this is so when there is no will whatever to murder, as, for instance, in the case of an unsuccessful operation. But it is possible to imagine an altogether different position: namely, when the will, though not setting the taking of human life as an objective, yet before the fact consents to murder, regarding murder here as an extreme and unavoidable measure. Would such a murder also be an absolute evil in your opinion?

PRINCE – Decidedly so, when once the will has agreed to a murder.

MR. Z. – You will admit, however, that there are cases in which the will, though agreeing to a murder, is at the same time not an "evil" will. The murder is consequently not an absolute evil in that case, even when looked at from this subjective side?

PRINCE – Oh, dear me! This is something quite unintelligible. But I think I guess what you mean: you refer to that famous case in which a father sees in a lonely place a blackguardly ruffian trying to assault his innocent (and, to enhance the effect, it is added, his "little") daughter. The father, unable to protect her in any other way, kills the offender. I have heard this argument at least a thousand times.

MR. Z. – What is really remarkable is not that you have heard it a thousand times, but the fact that nobody has ever had from any one of those holding your view a sensible, or even only plausible, answer to this simple argument.

PRINCE – And what is there in it to argue against?

MR. Z. – Well, if you don't like to argue against it, will

you then prove by some direct and positive method that, in all cases without exception and consequently in the case we are discussing, it is indisputably better to abstain from resisting evil by means of force than it is to use violence and risk the possibility of killing an albeit wicked and dangerous person.

PRINCE – It is funny to ask for a *special* proof of a single case. Once you recognize that murdering generally is evil in the moral sense, it is clear that it will be evil in every single case as well.

LADY – This sounds weak, Prince, I must say.

MR. Z. – Very weak indeed, I should say. That it is *generally* better not to kill anybody than to kill somebody is a truth which is not subject to argument and is accepted by all. It is only the single cases that actually raise the problem. The question is: Is the general and undisputed rule, "don't kill," unreservedly *absolute*? Does it therefore admit of *no* exceptions whatsoever, in *no* single case, under *no* circumstances? Or does the rule admit of even one exception, in which case it cannot be considered absolute?

PRINCE – I cannot agree to any such formal way of approaching the problem. I don't see the use of it. Suppose I admit that in your exceptional case, purposely invented for argument's sake —

LADY (*reprovingly*) – Prince! Prince! What is this I hear?

GENERAL (*ironically*) – Ho-ho-ho, Prince!

PRINCE (*taking no notice*) – Let us admit that, in your imaginary case, to kill is better than not to kill (in point of fact, of course, I refuse to admit it, but let us take for the moment that you are right). We may even take it that your case is not imaginary but quite real, though, as you will agree, it is extremely rare, exceptional . . . But here we are dealing with war, with something that is general, universal. Even you will not say that Napoleon, Moltke or Skobelev was in a position in any way resembling that of a father compelled to defend his innocent little daughter from the assaults of a monster. [3]

LADY – That's better! Bravo, *mon Prince!*

MR. Z. – A clever way, indeed, to avoid a difficult question. You will allow me, however, to establish the connection, logical as well as historical, that exists between these two facts — the single murder and the war. For this demonstration, let us again take your example, only we will strip it of the details which seem to increase, though actually they only diminish, its importance. We need not trouble ourselves about a father or a little daughter, for with them the problem at once loses its purely ethical meaning, being transferred from the sphere of intellectual and moral consciousness into that of natural moral feelings: parental love will obviously make the father kill the villain on the spot, without any further consideration as to whether he must or has the right to do so in the light of the higher moral ideal. So let us take not a father but a childless moralist before whose eyes some feeble being, strange and unfamiliar to him, is being fiercely assaulted by a cowardly villain. Would you suggest that the moralist should fold his arms and preach the glory of virtue while the fiendish beast is torturing his victim? Do you think the moralist will not feel a moral impulse to stop that beast by force, however great the possibility, or even the probability, of killing him may appear? And if instead he should permit the dastardly deed to take place to the accompaniment of his high-sounding phrases, don't you think that he would find no rest from his conscience and would feel ashamed of himself to the verge of repulsion?

PRINCE – Perhaps all that you are saying will be felt by a

[3] Helmuth Karl Bernhard von Moltke (1800–1891) reorganized Prussian army under Bismarck and devised strategic and tactical command methods for modern mass armies; Mikhail Dimitriyevich Skobelev (1843–82) distinguished himself as a Russian soldier — Translator.

moralist who does not believe in the reality of the good moral order, or who may have forgotten that God is not in might but in right.

LADY – Very well said, Prince. Now, Mr. Z., what will you answer to this?

MR. Z. – I will answer that I wish it was even better said — I mean more frankly, more simply, and more accurately. You wanted to say, did you not, that a moralist who really believes in the justice of God must, without forcibly interfering with the villain, pray to God that he should prevent the evil deed being carried out: either by a moral miracle, by suddenly turning the villain to the path of truth; or by a physical miracle, by an instantaneous paralysis, say, or —

LADY – No special need for a paralysis; the miscreant can be frightened by something, or in some other way prevented from carrying on his nefarious work.

MR. Z. – Oh, well, that makes no difference. The miracle lies, you understand, not so much in the fact itself as in the connection of that fact — be it a bodily paralysis or some mental excitement — with the prayer and its moral object. At any rate, the method suggested by the Prince is nothing else but a prayer for a miracle.

PRINCE – But . . . really . . . Why a prayer . . . and a miracle?

MR. Z. – What else then?

PRINCE – Well, if I believe that the world is governed by a beneficent and intelligent living power, I must also believe that whatever takes place in the world is in accord with that power, that is, with the will of God.

MR. Z. – Pardon me. How old are you?

PRINCE – Whatever do you mean by this question?

MR. Z. – Nothing offensive, I can assure you. I presume you are not less than thirty, are you?

PRINCE – Guess higher!

MR. Z. – So you must assuredly have had some occasion to see, or if not to see then to hear, or if not to hear then at least to read in the papers, that malicious and immoral things do happen in this world.

PRINCE – So?

MR. Z. – So? Does it not prove that neither "the moral order," the truth, nor the will of God — manifest themselves in the world by their own power?

POLITICIAN – Now we are getting down to business. If evil exists, the gods, it follows, either cannot or will not suppress it; and the gods, then, in the sense of omnipotent and beneficent powers, do not exist at all. Old, but true!

LADY – Oh, what awful things you are saying!

GENERAL – Talking leads to great discoveries! Only begin philosophizing and your feeble brain reels.

PRINCE – A poor philosophy this! As if the will of God were bound up with *our* ideas of what is good and evil.

MR. Z. – With *some* of our ideas it is not, but with the true notion of good it is bound up most firmly. On the other hand, if God is generally indifferent to good and evil, then you utterly refute your own argument.

PRINCE – How is that, I should like to know?

MR. Z. – Well, if you hold that God is not concerned when a powerful blackguard, swayed by his brute passions, crushes a poor feeble creature, then God is even more likely to have no objection if any one of us, actuated by human sympathy, crushes the blackguard. You will surely not attempt to defend the absurdity that only killing a weak and inoffensive being *is not* evil before the eyes of God, whereas killing a strong and wicked beast *is* evil.

PRINCE – It appears to you as an absurdity only because you look at it from the wrong point of view. From the moral standpoint the real importance attaches not to one who is killed, but to one who kills. Just now you yourself called the blackguard a beast, that is, a being lacking in intelligence and conscience. If this is the case, what evil can there be in his actions?

LADY – But don't you see that it is not a beast in the literal sense of the word as used here? It is as if I were to say to my daughter: "What nonsense you are talking about, my angel," and you were to get up and begin shouting at me: "How ridiculous a thing to say! How can angels talk nonsense?" Well, of course, all the arguments! . . .

PRINCE – Forgive me. I understand perfectly well that the villain is called a beast only in a metaphorical sense, and that this beast has neither tail nor hooves. But it is evident that the villain must literally lack intelligence and conscience; for a person with intelligence and conscience could not possibly commit such acts.

MR. Z. – Yet another play on words! Naturally, a person acting as a beast loses his intelligence and conscience in the sense that he is no longer moved by them. But that intelligence and conscience do not speak within him at all you still have to prove. Meanwhile, I continue to think that a bestial human being differs from me and you not by the absence of intelligence and conscience, but only by the willingness to act against them, and in accord with the impulse of the beast within him. Within every one of us lurks the beast, but we usually keep him tightly chained; the other person in question loosens the chain, only to be dragged along at its tail. He has the chain, but fails to make proper use of it.

GENERAL – Precisely. And, if the Prince still disagrees with you, he is hoist with his own petard! "The villain," the Prince says, "is only a beast without intelligence and conscience." Then killing him is the same as killing a wolf or a tiger springing at a human victim. Why, this sort of thing is permitted even by the Society for Prevention of Cruelty to Animals!"

PRINCE – But again you forget that whatever the state of mind of that person may be, whether completely devoid of intelligence and conscience, or whether consciously and willfully immoral, if such is possible, it is not that person who really matters, but you; *your* intelligence and conscience are not destroyed and *you* do not want consciously to go against their demands. Well then, you would not kill that individual, whatever he might have been.

MR. Z. – Naturally, I would not kill him should my intelligence and conscience absolutely forbid my doing so. Imagine, however, that intelligence and conscience tell me something entirely different — something which seems to be more sensible and morally correct.

PRINCE – This sounds interesting! Let us hear it.

MR. Z. – We may assume first of all that intelligence and conscience know how to count, at least, up to three . . .

GENERAL – Go on, go on!

MR. Z. – Therefore, intelligence and conscience, if they do not wish to lie to me, will not keep on telling me "two" when the actual number is "three" . . .

GENERAL (*impatiently*) – Well?

PRINCE – I can't see what he's driving at!

MR. Z. – Well, you assert, don't you, that intelligence and conscience speak to me only about myself and the villain? The whole point of your argument is that I should not lay a finger on him. But, in point of fact, there is present also a third person — who is actually the most important of all — the victim of the wicked assault, who requires my help. You always neglect the victim, but conscience speaks of the victim too, and even speaks of the victim in preference to the others. And if the will of God is involved here at all, it is only in the sense that I should save the victim, sparing the villain as much as possible — by persuasion, if it be possible; if not, by force. And should my hands be tied, *then* and only then can I call to my aid that *supreme* resource which was suggested by you too prematurely and then too lightly cast aside — the supreme resource of prayer, that is, an appeal to the Divine Intelligence, which,

I am sure, can really perform miracles when they are necessary. Which of these means of help should be used depends entirely on the internal and external conditions of the incident. The only absolute thing here is that I must help those who are wronged. That is what my conscience says.

GENERAL – The enemy's center is broken through! Hurrah!

PRINCE – My conscience has progressed beyond this elementary stage. In a case like this, my conscience tells me something more definite and concise: it says, *"Don't kill!"* and that is all. But I cannot see even now that we have moved any further in our argument. Suppose I agree with your proposition that *anyone*, even a morally cultured and truly conscientious person, could permit himself (or herself) to commit a murder, acting under the influence of sympathy and having no time to consider the moral character of his action — even admitting all this, I am still utterly unable to see what could follow from this admission that would enlighten us with regard to our principal problem. Let me ask you again: "Did Tamerlane, or Alexander the Great, or Lord Kitchener kill and make others kill people in order to protect weak, defenseless beings from the villainous assaults that were threatening them?"

MR. Z. – The juxtaposition of Tamerlane and Alexander the Great augurs ill for our historical accuracy, but since this is the second time that you have appealed to historical facts, allow me to quote an historical illustration that will really help us to compare the question of the defense of a person with that of a state. The affair happened in the twelfth century in Kiev. The feudal princes, who already then seemed to hold your ideas on war and believed that one may quarrel and fight only *chez soi*, would not agree to take the field against the Polovtsians, saying they were reluctant to subject their people to the horrors of war. To this the great Prince Vladimir Monomakh answered in the following words: "You pity the serf, but you forget that when spring comes the serf will go out to the field — "[4]

LADY – Please watch your language!

MR. Z. – But this is from a chronicle.

LADY – That makes no difference. I am sure you don't remember the chronicle by heart. You put it in your own words. It's all the same. It sounds so absurd. One hears "Spring will come" and expects "the flowers will blossom and the nightingales will sing," but instead all of a sudden comes "serf."[5]

MR. Z. – As you please, madam. But let me continue with the words of the great Prince Vladimir Monomakh. "The spring will come, the peasant will go out into the field with his horse to till the land. The Polovtsian will come, and will kill the peasant, and will take away his horse. Then a formidable band of Polovtsians will make an inroad, and will slaughter all the men, capture their wives and children, drive away their cattle, and burn out their homes. Can't you find it in your heart to pity the peasants for this? I do pity them, and for that reason I call upon you to take up arms against the Polovtsians." The feudal princes, ashamed of themselves, listened to his words, and the country enjoyed peace throughout the reign of Vladimir Monomakh. Afterward, however, they turned back to their "peaceful professions," which urged them to evade war with foreign enemies in order to carry on their miserable quarrels in the comfort of their own homes. The end of it all for Russia was the Mongolian yoke, and for the descen-

[4] Prince Vladimir Mononomakh (1053-1125) of Kiev tried to re-unite all of Russia in his campaign against the Polovtsians, the Russian name for a Mongolic-Turkish speaking people who clashed several times with the Russians in the eleventh and twelfth centuries — Translator.

[5] The equivalent Russian word "smerd" (serf, slave, etc.) suggests something stinking — Translator.

dants of these princes that rich feast of experience which history provided them in the person of Ivan the Terrible.

PRINCE – Your argument is absolutely beyond me! At one moment you describe an incident which has never happened to any one of us, and will certainly never occur in the future. At another moment you remind us of some Vladimir Monomakh, who perhaps never existed, and who, at any rate, has absolutely nothing to do with us . . .

LADY – *Parlez pour vous, monsieur!* Speak for yourself, sir!

MR. Z. – Tell me, Prince, are you a descendant of Rurik?

PRINCE – People say so. But do you suggest that I should for this reason take special interest in Rurik, Sineus, and Truvor? [6]

LADY – I think when one does not know one's ancestors one is little better than little boys and girls who believe that they were found in the garden under a cabbage leaf.

PRINCE – And what are those poor devils to do who have no ancestors?

MR. Z. – Everyone has at least two great ancestors who have bequeathed to posterity their circumstantial and highly instructive records: the history of one's country and that of the world.

PRINCE – But these records cannot decide for us how we should live *now*, and what we should *now* do. Let it be granted that Vladimir Monomakh actually existed, that he was not merely the creation of the imagination of the monk Laurentius, or of the monk Hypathius. [7] He may even have been an exceptionally good man, and he may have sincerely pitied the "serf." In such case he was right in fighting the Polovtsians, because in those barbaric times moral consciousness had not yet risen above the crude Byzantine

[6] The legendary founders of the Russian State — Translator.

[7] Writers of the Russian Chronicles, *Letopos'*, the first historical texts of Russian history — Editor.

notion of Christianity, and actually approved of murder when it was for a good purpose, real or imaginary. But how can we do so, when we have once understood that murder is an evil thing, opposed to the will of God and forbidden since the days of Moses by God's commandment? Under no guise nor name can killing ever become permissible for us. Still less can it cease to be evil when, instead of one man, thousands are slaughtered in the name of war. The whole thing is, in the first instance, a question of personal conscience.

GENERAL – Now that you reduce it all to personal conscience, allow me to tell you this much. I am a man who is in the moral sense (as in other senses, of course) of the average type: neither black nor white, but gray. I have never been guilty either of any extraordinary virtue or of any extraordinary villainy. Even when one performs good acts there are always grounds for self-suspicion. One can never say with certainty and candor what one's real motive is. The motive may be a real good, but again it may only be a weakness of the soul, or perhaps a habit of life, or even a personal vanity. Besides, all this is all so petty. In all my life there has been only one incident that, from the beginning, I could not call "petty", and what is more important, in which I am certain I was not guided by any doubtful motive but solely by the impulse of good that overcame me. Only once in my life did I experience complete moral satisfaction and even some kind of ecstasy, so that my actions were entirely free from considerations or hesitations. And this good act of mine has been to me till now, and will of course remain so forever, my very best and purest memory. Well, this single good act of mine was a murder, and not a little insignificant murder at that, for in some quarter of an hour I killed over a thousand men!

LADY – *Quelles blagues!* And I thought you were quite serious for once!

GENERAL – And so I am. I can produce witnesses if you

like. It was not with my own sinful hands that I killed, but with six pure, chaste steel guns, which poured forth a most virtuous and beneficent rain of shells.

LADY – Where was the good in that, I should like to know?

GENERAL – Though I am not only a soldier but in modern parlance a "militarist," it is needless to say that I would not call the mere annihilation of a thousand ordinary men a good act, were they Germans, or Hungarians, or Englishmen, or Turks. Here it was quite an exceptional case. Even now I cannot speak calmly about it, so painfully it stirred my soul.

LADY – Please do not keep us on tenterhooks. Tell us all about it.

GENERAL – I mentioned guns. You will then have guessed that the affair happened in the last Russo-Turkish war. I was with the Caucasian army after October 3 —.

LADY – What about October 3?

GENERAL – That was the day of the last great battle in the Aladja mountains when, for the first time, we crushed all the ribs of the "invincible" Hasi-Moukhtar Pasha. Afterward we at once advanced into Asiatic country. I was on the left front at the head of the advance guard engaged in scouting. I had under me the Nijny-Novgorod Dragoons, three "sotnia" of Kuban Cossacks, and a battery of horse artillery. The country was not particularly inspiring: in the mountains it was fairly decent, sometimes even beautiful. But down in the valleys nothing but deserted, burned-out villages and downtrodden fields were to be seen. One morning — October 28, it was — we were descending a valley where, according to the map, there was a big Armenian village. As a matter of fact, there was no village to be seen, though there really had been one there not long before, and of a decent size, too; its smoke could be seen miles away. I had my detachment well together in close formation, for reports had been received that we might run into a strong cavalry force. I was riding with the Dragoons; the Cossacks were in advance. There was a sharp bend in the road as we neared the village. Suddenly the Cossacks reined in their horses and stood as if rooted to the spot. I galloped forward. Before I could see anything I guessed by the smell of roasting flesh that the Bashi-Bazouks [8] had left their "kitchen" behind. A huge caravan of Armenian refugees had not been able to escape in time. The crowd had been caught by the Turks, who had "made a good job of it" in their own inimitable fashion. They had bound the poor Armenians, some by the head, some by the feet, some by the waist, to high cart axles, had lit fires underneath, and had slowly grilled them. Dead women lay here and there — some with breasts cut off, others with abdomens ripped open. I need not go into further particulars. But one scene will remain forever vivid in my memory. A poor woman lay there on the ground, her head and shoulders securely bound to the cart's axle, so that she could not move her head. She bore no burns, no wounds. But on her distorted face was stamped a ghastly terror — she had evidently died of sheer horror. And before her dead, staring eyes was a high pole, firmly fixed in the ground, and to it was tied the poor little naked body of a baby — her son, most likely — a blackened, scorched little corpse, with protruding eyes. Nearby also was a grating in which lay the dead ashes of a fire . . . I was overcome by a deadly grief, it was repulsive to look at this God's earth, and my actions became mechanical. I bade my men to put their horses to the gallop. We entered the burned village; it was razed to the ground; not a house remained. Presently we saw a poor wretch crawling out of a dry well. He was covered with mud; his clothes were in rags. He fell on his knees, and began wailing something in Armenian. We helped him to his feet, and plied him with eager questions. He proved to be an

[8] Turkish mercenaries — Editor.

Armenian from a distant village, a fairly intelligent fellow. He had come to the place on business just as the inhabitants had decided to flee. They had hardly started off when the Bashi-Bazouks fell upon them — an immense number, he said, at least forty thousand. He wasn't, of course, in any condition to count. He managed to hide himself in the well. He heard the cries of the tortured people; he knew full well what was happening. Later, he heard the Bashi-Bazouks come back and go off again by a different route. "They were going to my own village," he groaned, "and then they will do the same terrible things to all our folk." The poor wretch moaned pitifully, wringing his hands in despair. At that moment an inspiration seemed suddenly to come to me. My agony of soul seemed suddenly comforted. God's world became once more a happy place to dwell in. I quietly asked the Armenian how long it was since those devils had left the place. He reckoned it about three hours.

"And how long would it take for a horse to get to your village?"

"Over five hours."

No, it was impossible to overtake them in two hours. What a damnable business!

"Do you know of another and shorter way to your place?" I asked.

"I do, sir, I do." And he became at once excited. "There is a way across the defile. It is very short. And only a few people know it."

"Is it passable on horseback?"

"It is, sir."

"And for artillery?"

"It would be rather difficult, but it could be done, sir."

I ordered my men to supply the Armenian with a horse, and with all my detachment followed him into the defile. How we all seemed to crawl there among the mountains; yet I hardly seemed to notice anything by the way. Once more my actions had become merely mechanical. But in the depths of my soul I felt utter and complete confidence. I knew *what* I had to do, and I felt that it *would* be done. My heart was light; I flew on wings; I exulted in the certain fulfillment of my plans.

We were already filing out from the last defile, after which we should come to the high road, when I saw our Armenian galloping back and waving his hands frantically, as if to say, "Here they are!" I caught up with the advance guard, and leveling my telescope I could see that he was right. I saw an apparently endless column of horses — not forty thousand, of course, but three or four thousand at least, if not even five. These sons of devils at once spotted the Cossacks and turned to meet them. We were coming out of the defile against their left front. A hail of bullets greeted the Cossacks. These Asiatic monsters could fire their European guns like real human beings. Here and there a Cossack was picked off by a shot. A Cossack officer rode up to me and shouted: "Order the attack, sir. Why should these beasts be allowed to shoot us like quails, while we are mounting our artillery? We can put them to flight ourselves."

"Patience, my dear fellow, for just one little moment," I told him. "I have no doubt that you would be able to put them to flight; but what would be the pleasure of that? God bids me to wipe them out and not drive them away." Here I ordered two "sotnia" of Cossacks advancing in open order to let fly at the devils, and later, when well in the thick of it, to retreat on the battery. One hundred Cossacks I left to mask the guns, while the Nijny-Novgorod men were placed in phalanx to the left of the battery. I trembled with impatience. The burnt child with its protruding eyes came vividly before me. The Cossacks were falling, shot! God!

Lady – And the end?

General – The end came just fine, without a hitch. The Cossacks engaging the enemy presently began their retreat, yelling wildly in their usual fashion. Those sons of devils came pell-mell after them, too excited even to open fire, and galloping en masse on our position. Within four hundred yards of our line the Cossacks suddenly scattered, each man seeking cover where he could. "At last," I felt, "God's hour has struck!" I turned to the squad of Cossacks covering the guns. "Cossacks! Wheel!" I shouted. The covering squad divided, right and left, leaving the battery unmasked. Lord bless us! Then I gave the word "Fire!"

And the Lord did bless fully and completely each one of my six charges. Never in my life have I heard such a devilish yell. They did not come to their senses even when the second volley of shells smote them, cutting red lanes through and through.

Suddenly the horde wheeled. A third volley followed them up! What a bloody mess it made! Have you seen an ants' nest, on which burning matches have been thrown? — the ants all rushing about, crushing each other? . . . In a moment our Cossacks and Dragoons had charged them on the left flank, cutting, hacking, and slicing them like cabbage. Few of them managed to get away; those who escaped the rain of shells were cut down by the sabers. Some threw their guns away, jumped off their horses, and whined for mercy. But I was past giving orders. My men understood well enough that it was not a time for mercy. So the Cossacks and the men of Nijny-Novgorod sabered them to a man.

Yet it is a sure thing that if these brainless Satans, after the first two volleys were fired point-blank into their midst at a range of about forty to sixty yards, instead of rushing back had galloped on the battery, there would have been an end to all of us — no third volley would have been fired . . . Well, God was with us. The whole thing was over. And in my soul I felt the joy and peace of an Easter Sunday! We gathered our slain — thirty-seven men gave up their souls to God. We laid them together on the level ground in rows, and closed their eyes. I had an old sergeant in the third "sotnia", Odarchenko by name, an earnest student of the Bible and singularly gifted. In England he would have become a Prime Minister. Now he is in Siberia, banished for resisting the authorities when they were shutting up some "old believers'" monastery and destroying the tomb of one of their sainted elders. I called him. "Well, Odarchenko," I said, "now that we are in the field there is no time for arguing about the 'hallelujahs,' so you be our priest and perform the funeral service over our dead." For him this was, of course, a heaven-sent opportunity. "I shall be only too glad to do it, sir," he replied, and the face of the little creature fairly beamed with joy. There was also a rough-and-ready choir. The service was performed with all ceremony. Only the absolution was lacking, but this was not necessary either: their sins were already remitted by the words of Christ himself about those who "lay down their lives for their friends." Even now I can see the ceremony vividly before my eyes. The day had been cloudy, as it usually was in the autumn season, but at that moment the sky was clearing before the setting sun, and above the dark loom of the gloomy defile rose- and amber-tinted clouds were gathering like God's own regiments. My soul was still in ecstasy with the glory of our fight. Wondrous peace rested upon me. I felt that all worldly stains were washed away, and that all the burden of earthly trouble had fallen from my shoulders. I was in Paradise — I was feeling God, and there was the end of it. And when Odarchenko started calling out the names of the departed warriors who on the battlefield had laid down their lives for their faith, their Tsar, and their fatherland, I truly felt that verily there was such a thing as a Christ-loving band of warriors, and that it was no mere official expression, no mere empty title, as you were pleased to call it. I felt that war is, as it was then, is now, and ever will be till the ending of the world, something great, honorable, and holy . . .

PRINCE (*after a short interval of silence*) – Well, when you buried your men in your happy frame of mind, tell me, didn't you think at all of the enemies whom you had killed in such great numbers?

GENERAL – Thank God,we were able to move further before that carrion had time to remind us of itself.

LADY – Ah, now you have spoiled the whole impression. What a shame!

GENERAL (*addressing the Prince*) – And what would you have me do? Give Christian burial to those jackals, who were neither Christians nor Moslems, but the Devil knows what? Imagine for a moment that I went out of my senses and ordered the service to be performed over them, together with the Cossacks. In that case would you not charge me with intolerance? To think of it! These poor dead fellows, when alive, worshipped the Devil and prayed to the fire, and now after their death they are suddenly to be subjected to superstitious and crude pseudo-Christian rites! No, I had something else to worry about. I called all the officers and ordered them to tell the men that not one of them should dare to come within ten yards of the damned carrion. I could well see that my Cossacks' fingers itched to search the pockets of those killed, as was their habit. And who knows what plague might have spread as a result? Let the Devil take the lot of them.

PRINCE – Do I understand you correctly? You were afraid lest the Cossacks should begin robbing the dead Bashi-Bazouks and should carry from them some infectious disease to your force?

GENERAL – That is exactly what I feared. I think the point is clear enough.

PRINCE – What a Christ-loving band of warriors!

GENERAL – Who, the Cossacks? They are veritable brigands! They always were.

PRINCE – But, really, what is all this? Are we talking in dreams?

GENERAL – It seems to me that there must be something wrong. I can't make out what it is that you really want to know.

POLITICIAN – The Prince is probably surprised that your ideal and all but canonized Cossacks all of a sudden prove, in your own words, to be "veritable" brigands!

PRINCE – That's it. And I ask you, how can war be "something great, honorable, and holy," when you admit yourself that it is a struggle between one group of brigands and another?

GENERAL – Now I see your point. "A struggle of one group of brigands with another." But don't you see that the *other* brigands are of quite a different sort? Or do you really believe that to rob when occasion offers itself is the same as to roast little babies before the eyes of their mothers? Well, I'll tell you this much. So clear is my conscience in this matter that even now I sometimes regret with all my soul that I did not die after I had given the order to fire the last volley. I have not the slightest doubt that should I have died then, I should have gone before the Throne of God with all my thirty-seven slain Cossacks, and we would have taken our places in Paradise by the side of the Good Thief. It was not for nothing that the Bible placed him there, was it?

PRINCE – That is true. But you will certainly not find it written in the Bible that only people of our own country or of our own religion can be likened to the Good Thief, and not people of all nationalities and creeds.

GENERAL – Upon my word, you could not place more misstatements to my credit if I were already dead! When have I made distinctions among nations and creeds? Are Armenians my countrymen and coreligionists? Or have I referred to the faith and nationality of the devil's spawn that I annihilated with shells?

PRINCE – But you fail to remember the fact that the aforesaid "devil's spawn" are, after all, human beings, that in every man you can find both good and evil, and that every brigand, be he a Cossack or a Bashi-Bazouk, might yet prove to be a "good thief."

GENERAL – How am I to take you? At one moment you say that an evil man is like an irresponsible beast, at another moment you state that a Bashi-Bazouk roasting babies might well prove to be a good thief. And all because you fear to touch evil with even a finger! For me the important point is not that every man has within him the seeds of both good and evil, but which of the two — good or evil — has taken firmer root in him. It matters little that wine and vinegar are both made from the juice of the grape. What is of real importance is whether a certain bottle has wine or vinegar in it. Because should it be vinegar and I begin drinking it glass after glass, and treat others to it simply because it happens to be made from the same material as wine, I am pretty certain that this exhibition of my cleverness would not do anybody any good at all. On the contrary, it may ruin good digestions! Now, all men are brothers. Very good. I am glad to hear it. But how far will this take us? There are different kinds of brothers, you know. Why, then, should I not be inquisitive enough to find out which of my brothers is Cain and which is Abel? And suppose I happen to see my brother Cain flaying my brother Abel, and because all men are brothers I deal out such a blow to my brother Cain as will teach him to give up forever his bad habits. Will you then come out and blame me for forgetting that all three of us are brothers? Of course, I don't forget it. Why, it is only because I remember this brotherhood that I interfere at all. Otherwise I could pass by and take no notice.

PRINCE – But why those alternatives — either passing by or dealing a blow?

GENERAL – No third issue can generally be found in such cases. You have been suggesting praying to God that he should personally interfere and by the might of his own right hand bring every devil's son to his senses. But you yourself cast this idea aside, didn't you? I admit willingly that prayer is good in all circumstances, but it cannot be substituted for action on one's own part. Pious people, for instance, say prayers even before they have their meals, but they have to do their chewing themselves, and with their own jaws. Nor did I give orders to my horse artillery without saying my prayers!

PRINCE – Such prayers are blasphemy, of course. It is not praying to God that is necessary, but acting according to God's will.

GENERAL – For example?

PRINCE – One who is imbued with the true Christian spirit will, in the hour of need, find within himself the power to influence a poor ignorant brother who is about to commit a murder or some other evil. By means of words and gestures, and even by his very looks, the true Christian will be able to make such a startling impression upon the mind of the wrongdoer that he will instantly see his error and will forsake the ways of evil.

GENERAL – Holy saints! Is it before the Bashi-Bazouks, who roasted babies, that you think I should have performed all the touching gestures and said these moving words?

MR. Z. – Words, perhaps, would not have been quite appropriate owing to the distance intervening and to the fact that neither of you understood the other's language. And as to gestures making a startling impression — say what you will, nothing could have been more fitting in the circumstances than the rounds of shells fired.

LADY – Really, in what language and with the help of what instruments could the General make himself understood by the Bashi-Bazouks?

PRINCE – I have never said that *they* could have impressed the Bashi-Bazouks in the Christian way. What I did say was that a person full of the true Christian spirit would have found some means, even in this case as in every other, to awaken in those dark souls the good which lies hidden in every human being.

MR. Z. – Do you really believe in this?

PRINCE – I have not the slightest doubt about it.

MR. Z. – Well, do you think, then, that Christ was *sufficiently* imbued with this "true Christian spirit," or not?

PRINCE – What a strange question to ask!

MR. Z. – I ask it only to learn from you why it was that Christ could not use the power of the Christian spirit to such effect as to awaken the good hidden in the souls of Judas, Herod, the priests of the Sanhedrin, and, lastly, of that *evil* thief, who usually remains entirely forgotten when his *good* comrade is mentioned. There is no insuperable difficulty here for positive Christian thought. But you are obliged to sacrifice one of two things: either your habit of quoting Christ and the Bible as the highest authority, or your moral optimism. Because the third path, which has been rather too much hackneyed — that of denying the very facts of the New Testament as a later invention or a mere priestly commentary — in the present case is entirely taken from you. However much you mutilate and edit the text of the four Gospels to suit your object, this fact, principal for our argument will remain: namely, that Christ suffered cruel persecutions and the tortures of crucifixion at the hands of malicious enemies. That personally he remained morally above all this spite, that he forgave them — all this is equally easy to understand, both from my point of view and from yours. Then why is it that, forgiving his enemies, he — to use your own words — "did not save their souls" from the cloud of ignorance in which they were enwrapped? Why didn't He conquer their spite by the power of his benignity? Why didn't he awaken the good that lay dormant in them, and give enlightenment and new life to their souls? In short, why didn't he impress Judas, Herod, and the Sanhedrin in the same way in which he impressed the *single* good thief? It follows that he could not do so, or did not wish to do so. In either case, however, *according to your argument*, Christ must have been *insufficiently* imbued with the "true Christian spirit"! On which conclusion I beg you to accept my hearty congratulations.

PRINCE – Oh! I refuse to fence with you in a duel of words, just as I refused to engage in combat with the General, using for weapons his "Christ-loving" swords.

(Here the Prince stood up, evidently on the point of saying something strong enough to flatten his opponent at a blow, and without fencing at all; but the bells of a neighboring church struck the hour of seven.)

LADY – It's time to have dinner. But a discussion like this should not be finished hurriedly. After dinner we play whist, but tomorrow this conversation certainly must be continued. (*Addressing the Politician*) Do you agree?

POLITICIAN – To the continuation of this discussion? I am only too glad it has come to an end! This argument has acquired much of the unpleasant quality of a religious war, not at all befitting the season of the year. Besides, my life is the most precious thing to me.

LADY – It is no good pretending. You must, you must certainly take part in the rest of the discussion. You ought to be ashamed of yourself — a Mephistopheles in secret, sprawling luxuriously on a sofa!

POLITICIAN – Very well, then. I have no objection to resuming the discussion tomorrow, but only on the condition that religion is kept out of it as much as possible. I do not demand that it should be banished altogether — that seems to be impossible. But, for God's sake, let us have as little of it as we can.

LADY – Your "for God's sake" is very sweet in this connection.

MR. Z. (*to the Politician*) – I think the best way to have as little religion as possible would be for you to monopolize the conversation!

POLITICIAN – I will, I promise you, although it is always more pleasant to listen than to speak, particularly in this healthy air. But to save our little company from the contentious struggle which may perniciously reflect upon the whist too, I am willing to sacrifice myself for two hours.

LADY – How delightful of you! And on the day after tomorrow we will have the rest of our discussion on the Bible. The Prince will by that time prepare some absolutely irrefutable argument. But you must be present too. After all, one should learn at least a little of matters ecclesiastical!

POLITICIAN – The day after tomorrow too? Oh, no! My self-sacrifice does not go so far as that! Besides, I have to go to Nice on that day.

LADY – To Nice? What a transparent pretext! It is useless, I assure you, for we saw through you long ago. Everybody knows that when a man says, "I have an appointment in Nice," he really proposes a bit of fun at Monte Carlo. Well, let it be so. After tomorrow we must manage somehow to do without you. Plunge yourself to the neck in pleasure — that is, if you are not afraid of becoming soon a ghost yourself. Go to Monte Carlo. And may Providence reward you according to your deserts.

POLITICIAN – My deserts do not concern *Providence*, but only the *provision* of certain necessary measures I have carried out for the benefit of society. But I admit the influence of luck and the value of a little calculation in roulette as well as in everything else.

LADY – Tomorrow, however, we must all meet here without fail.

CHAPTER TWO
THE SECOND CONVERSATION
Audiatur et altera *pars*

Next afternoon, at the appointed hour, we were having tea under the palm trees. Only the Prince was late; we had to wait for him. As I did not play cards that evening, I was able to take down the whole of the second discussion from the beginning. This time the Politician spoke at length, drawling out interminable, intricate sentences. I was unable to write down his exact words. I do quote verbatim some of what he said, making an attempt to preserve his characteristic utterance; but more often I give only the substance of his speech in my own words.

POLITICIAN – For some time now I have been observing an extraordinary fact: people who pretend to take a vast interest in certain of the higher morals never seem able to exercise the simplest, the most necessary, and, in my opinion, the one essential virtue — politeness. All the more reason, therefore, to thank the Creator that we have comparatively few individuals obsessed with this notion of a higher morality. I say "notion," because, as a matter of fact, I have never come across these "higher morals", and therefore have no reason to believe in their actual existence.

LADY – There is nothing new in that. As to politeness, there is some truth in what you say. Therefore, before we approach the main subject of our discussion, perhaps you will attempt a proof that politeness is the one essential virtue. A trial proof, let us say, on which you may test your powers just as musicians test their instruments in the orchestra before the overture.

powers just as musicians test their instruments in the orchestra before the overture.

POLITICIAN – When the orchestra is tuning up, we hear only single disconnected sounds. I fear my proof would inflict on us a similar monotony; for hardly anyone would urge the opposite opinion — at least, not before the Prince comes in. Of course, once he arrives it would not be at all polite to speak of politeness.

LADY – Obviously. But what are your arguments?

POLITICIAN – I think you will agree that it would be quite possible to live an enjoyable life in a society in which there was not a single person chaste, or disinterested, or unselfish. I, at any rate, have always lived in such society without feeling in the least uncomfortable.

LADY – In Monte Carlo for instance?

POLITICIAN – In Monte Carlo, or anywhere else. Nowhere is there any need for a single exponent of the higher morals. But try to live in company where you cannot find a single polite person!

GENERAL – I don't know what kinds of company you are talking about, but in the Khiva campaign [1] or in the Turkish campaign we should have fared ill if we had no other virtue than politeness.

POLITICIAN – You may just as well say that something besides politeness is necessary for travelers in Central Africa. I am speaking of ordinary, everyday life in a civilized human society. For a civilized life no higher virtues and no Christianity, so called, are necessary. (*To Mr. Z.*) You shake your head?

MR. Z. – I have just recollected a sad incident, of which I was told the other day.

LADY – What was it?

MR. Z. – My friend N. died suddenly.

---

[1] A play upon words in Russian; the word for "company" is the same as the word for "campaign" — Translator.

GENERAL – Is he the well-known novelist?

MR. Z. – That's the man.

POLITICIAN – The notices about his death in the press were rather obscure.

MR. Z. – Obscure they were, indeed.

LADY – But what made you think of him just at this moment? Was he killed by somebody's impoliteness?

MR. Z. – Not at all! He died because of his own excessive politeness and nothing else.

GENERAL – Once more, it seems, it is impossible for us to agree.

LADY – Tell us the story, please, if you can.

MR. Z. – There is nothing to conceal in it. My friend believed that politeness, if not the only virtue, is at least the first inevitable stage of social morality. He regarded it as his duty to carry out all its prescriptions in the strictest possible way. For instance, he held politeness, among other things, to include the reading of all the letters he received, even those sent by strangers, and also of all the books and pamphlets sent him with demands for reviews. He scrupulously answered every letter and as scrupulously wrote all the reviews demanded by his correspondents. He complied with all the requests and responded to all the appeals made to him. As a result he found himself busy all day long attending to other people's affairs, and for his own work he had to be satisfied with the nighttime. More than this, he accepted every invitation and saw all the visitors who caught him at home. So long as my friend was young and could easily stand the effects of frequent strong potations, this galley-slave existence he created for himself because of his politeness merely annoyed him, and did not lead to tragedy: wine brought joy to his heart and saved him from despair. When he felt he would hang himself rather than stand it any longer, he would fetch out a bottle, from which he drew that which helped him drag his chains more cheerfully. But he was by no means a robust man, and at the age of forty-five had to give up drinking strong liquors. In his new state of sobriety he found his hard labor to be hell itself, and now I am told that he has committed suicide.

LADY – Do you mean to say that this was the result solely of his politeness?

MR. Z. – I have no doubt that the poor fellow had lost his spiritual and mental balance. But the word "simply" I think is hardly applicable to his case.

GENERAL – I, too, have known similar cases of madness. They would drive us mad too if we cared to examine them carefully: there is precious little that is simple about them.

POLITICIAN – One thing is clear, however, and that is, politeness has nothing to do with the case. Just as the Spanish Throne is not responsible for the madness of Councillor Popristchin,[2] so the duty of politeness is not answerable for the madness of your friend.

MR. Z. – I quite agree. I am by no means opposed to politeness, I merely object to making it into some kind of absolute rule.

POLITICIAN – An absolute rule, like everything else absolute, is only an invention of those who are lacking in common sense and the feeling of reality. There are no absolute rules for me. I recognize only *necessary* rules. For instance, I know perfectly well that if I disregard the rules of cleanliness the result will be unpleasant to myself and to everyone else. As I have no desire to experience any objectionable sensations myself or to make other people experience them, I invariably observe the rule of washing myself daily, of changing my linen, and so forth, not because this is recognized by others, or by myself, or because it is something sacred which it is a sin to disregard, but simply because any disregard of this rule would be *ipso facto* materially inconvenient. The same applies to politeness in general, which, properly speaking, includes cleanli-

2 The hero of Gogol's *The Diary of a Madman* — Translator.

ness as a part of it. It is much more convenient for me, as for everybody else, to observe rather than to break the rules of politeness. So I follow them. It suited your friend's fancy to imagine that politeness required from him that he answer all letters and requests without considering his personal comforts and advantage. That sort of thing is surely not politeness at all, but merely an absurd kind of self-denial.

MR. Z. – An abnormally developed conscientiousness gradually became with him a mania, which eventually brought him to his ruin.

LADY – But it is awful that a man should have died because of such a foolish idea. How is it that you could not bring him to his senses?

MR. Z. – I tried my best and had a powerful ally in a pilgrim from Mount Athos. He, by the way, was one of "God's fools" himself, but he had a remarkable personality all the same. My friend thought highly of him and often asked his advice in spiritual matters. The pilgrim instantly perceived the root of the evil. I know the man very well and I was sometimes present at their conversations. When my friend began telling him of his moral doubts and asking whether he was right in this or wrong in that, Barsanophius would immediately interrupt him with: "What, distressed about your sins? Give it up, my dear fellow, it is nothing. Let me tell you this: sin five hundred and thirty-nine times a day if you like, but, for Heaven's sake, don't repent. To sin first and then to repent? Why, anybody can do that. Sin, by all means — and often! But repent? Never! For if sin is evil then to remember sin is to be vindictive, and nobody approves of that. The worst vindictiveness of all is to remember your own sins. It is far better to remember the evil done to you by others — there would be some benefit in that, as you would be careful with such people in the future. But as for your own sins — forget them utterly. It is by far the better way. There is only one mortal sin —

despondency, because it gives birth to despair, and despair is not even a sin, it is the death of spirit itself. Now, what other sins are there? Drunkenness? But a clever man drinks only so much as he has room for. If he has no room left, he leaves off drinking. A fool can get drunk even on spring water. So you see the real cause lies not in the strength of the wine, but in the weakness of the human being. Some people are absolutely scorched up with vodka, and not only internally, but externally as well. They become completely black and little flashes of blue flame flicker all over them; I have seen this with my own eyes. How can you speak of the presence of sin when all the time hell itself is visibly coming out from you? And as to transgressions of the seventh commandment, let me tell you candidly that it is as difficult to censure them as it is impossible to praise them. But I can hardly recommend them! There is ecstatic pleasure in it — that one cannot deny — but at the end it brings despondency and shortens one's life. If you don't believe me, see what a learned German doctor writes." Here Barsanophius would take an old-fashioned book from a shelf and would begin turning over the pages. "The title alone is worth something, my dear fellow," he would say. "*The Macrobiotica*, by Hufeland! Look here, page 176." And he would slowly read passages in which the German doctor earnestly warns his readers against extravagant waste of the vital forces. "You see? Why then should a clever person suffer any loss? While one is young and thoughtless the imagination pictures all sorts of things. But later on — no, it is too costly an amusement. And as for recalling the past and grieving over it and sighing 'Alas! why have I damned myself? I have lost my innocence and spotted the purity of my soul and body!' This, I can assure you, is mere foolishness. It simply means that you deliver yourself right into the hands of the Devil for his eternal amusement. It flatters him, naturally, that your soul cannot go forward and upward, but stays marking time in the same old filthy spot.

Here is my advice to you: as soon as the Devil starts disturbing you by this sort of repentance, you simply spit and rub the spit with your foot, saying, 'See now, all my grievous sins, here they are. Ah, what a lot they mean to me. What rot!' I can assure you the Devil will leave you alone then. I speak from experience . . . Well, what other sins have you got? Are you thinking of trying stealing? If you did steal, well, there is no very great harm in that: nowadays everybody steals. You mustn't think anything at all of such a trifle. The one thing to beware of is despondency. Should the memory of your past sins torment you, so that you wonder whether you have done harm to anybody or anything, go to a theatre, or join some jolly friends, or read something funny. And if a rule is what you want, here it is: Be firm in your faith, not through fear of sins, but because it is a joyful thing for an intelligent person to live with God; without God a person is utterly wretched. Try to understand the word of God. If you read it carefully there is comfort and happiness in every verse. Say your prayers with a real uplifting of your soul once or twice a day. Do you ever forget to wash yourself? No? Well, a sincere prayer is better for a person's soul than any amount of soap is for his body. Fast for the health of the stomach and your other organs. Every doctor prescribes this for people on the wrong side of forty. Don't worry about other people's business. And don't go in for organized charity, if you have your own occupation. But give alms to the poor you meet, and never stay to count the cost. Give without stint to churches and monasteries. Do not reckon the amount. In heaven's clearinghouse they will count it all up themselves. Then you will be healthy in body and soul. As for those hypocrites who would poke their noses into everybody's soul, because they find their own so hollow, don't even speak to them."

Such talks as these had a very beneficial effect on my

poor friend, but they could not raise him from the mire of despondency; and at the end he seldom met Barsanophius.

POLITICIAN – Do you know that this pilgrim of yours says in his own way essentially what I have been saying?

LADY – So much the better. What a wonderful moralist he is, indeed! "Sin, if you must, but above all never repent." It appeals to me mightily!

GENERAL – I suppose that he does not talk like this to everyone? In dealing with a murderer or a scoundrel he must surely adopt a quite different tone.

MR. Z. – That should be obvious. But as soon as he observes a person overwhelmed with moral doubts he at once becomes a philosopher and even a fatalist. He once delighted a very clever and educated old lady. Though she was Russian by faith, she was educated abroad, and having heard a great deal about our Barsanophius, she looked to him as to *un directeur de conscience*. Barsanophius, however, did not allow her to talk too much about the worries of her soul. "Why do you worry yourself about all this rubbish? Who wants to hear it? I am only a common peasant, and yet it bores me to death. How can you imagine, then, that God can take any interest in it? And what is the good of talking about it? You are too old and too weak to begin improvement now." She herself recounted this conversation to me, laughing and weeping at the same time. True, she tried to argue with him, but he completely persuaded her by a story from the life of two ancient hermits — a story Barsanophius told me and N. very often. It is a fine story, only it will perhaps take too long to tell it.

LADY – Tell us in brief.

MR. Z. – Two hermits had gone out into the Nitrian Desert to save their souls. Their caves were not far distant from each other, but they themselves never talked together, except that they occasionally sang psalms, so that they could hear each other. In this way they spent many years, and their fame began to spread in Egypt and the surrounding countries. It came to pass that one day the Devil managed to put into both their minds simultaneously one and the same desire, and without saying a word to each other they collected their work baskets and mats made of palm leaves and branches, and went off to Alexandria. They sold their work there, and then for three days and three nights they sought pleasure in the company of drunkards and sinners, after which they went back to their desert.

And one of them cried out in bitterness and agony of the soul: "I am lost eternally! Cursed am I! No prayers and penance can atone for such madness, such abominations! All my years of fasting and prayer gone for nothing! I am ruined, body and soul!"

The other man, however, was walking by his side, singing psalms in a cheerful voice.

"Brother," said the repentant one, "have you gone mad?"

"Why do you ask that?"

"But why aren't you grieving?"

"What should I grieve about?"

"Listen to him! Have you forgotten Alexandria?"

"What about Alexandria? Glory to God who preserves that famous and God-fearing city!"

"But we, what did we do in Alexandria?"

"You know well enough yourself what we did; we sold our baskets, worshipped St. Mark, visited other churches, called on the pious governor of the city, conversed with the good prioress Leonilla who is always kind to monks . . ."

"But didn't we spend the night in a house of ill fame?"

"God save us! No! We spent the evening and the night in the patriarch's court."

"Holy martyrs! He has lost his mind . . . Where then did we treat ourselves to wine?"

"We partook of wine and food at the patriarch's table on the occasion of the Presentation of the Blessed Virgin."

"Poor, miserable creature! And who was it whom we kissed, not to mention worse things?"

"We were honored with a holy kiss on departing by the holy father of fathers, the most blessed Archbishop of the great city of Alexandria and of all Egypt, Libya and Pentapolis, and Judge of the World, Cyrus-Timotheus, with all the fathers and brothers of his divinely appointed clergy."

"Are you making a fool of me? Or has the Devil himself entered your soul as punishment for yesterday's abominations? They were wretched libertines, you blackguard, that you kissed!"

"Well, I don't know which of us the Devil has entered: Whether he has entered me, who am rejoicing in the gifts of God and in the benevolence of the godly priests, and am praising my Creator, as should every other living thing — or whether he has entered you, who are now raving like a lunatic and calling the house of our blessed father and pastor a house of ill fame, all the time insulting him and his God-loving clergy by calling them libertines."

"Oh, you heretic! You offspring of Arian! Accursed mouth of Apollinarius!"

At this the hermit who had been grieving over his lapse from virtue fell upon his comrade and began beating him with all his might. When the outburst was over, they returned silently to their caves. All night long the repentant one wore himself out with grief, filling the desert with his groans and cries, tearing out his hair, throwing himself on the ground and dashing his head against it, while the other quietly and happily sang his psalms. Next morning the repentant one was struck by a sudden thought: "By my many years of self-denial I had been granted a special blessing of the Holy Spirit which had already begun to reveal itself in miracles and apparitions. And if *after this* I gave myself up to the abominations of the flesh, I must have committed a sin against the Holy Spirit, which, according to the word of God, is for all eternity unpardonable. I cast a pearl, pure as heaven, before the swine of my reason — those devils — and they have crushed it to powder. Now they will most certainly turn on me and tear me to pieces. If, however, I am irrevocably doomed, what can I do here in the desert?" And so he went to Alexandria and gave himself up to a wanton life. It so happened that soon afterward he badly needed money, and, in company with other dissolute fellows like himself, murdered and robbed a wealthy merchant. The crime was discovered; he was tried by the city court, sentenced to death, and died an unrepentant sinner.

At the same time his old friend, continuing his life of devotion, attained to the highest degree of saintliness and became famous for his great miracles. By the virtue of his word alone, women who had no children for many years gave birth to male offspring. When finally the day of his death arrived, his decrepit and withered body suddenly became resplendent with the beauty of youth. A wondrous light surrounded it; from it proceeded the perfume of sweet spices. After his death a monastery was constructed over his relics, and his name passed from the Alexandrian church to the Byzantine, and thence to the church calendars of Kiev and Moscow. "It proves that I am telling the truth," Barsanophius used to say in conclusion, "When I say that there is only one sin which does harm, and that is despondency." The pilgrims both committed every other crime, but only one met his doom — the one who became despondent.

GENERAL – You see, even monks have to be cheerful; whereas nowadays some would like to cover even our soldiers with despondency.

MR. Z. – After all, then, though we have departed from the question of politeness, we have nevertheless again approached our main subject.

LADY – And just at the right moment. For here comes the

Prince at last. We have been talking, in your absence, about politeness.

PRINCE – Please forgive me; I could not get here earlier. A bundle of all sorts of papers from our people, and various parcels of books, arrived. I'll show you them by and by.

LADY – Very well. Later too, I will tell you the legend of the two monks with which we have been consoling ourselves in your absence. At present our Privy Monte Carlist holds the floor. Let us now hear what he has to say about war following our discussion yesterday.

POLITICIAN – From yesterday's conversation I have retained in my memory Mr. Z.'s reference to Vladimir Monomakh, and the war story told by the General. Let these be our starting points for further discussion of the question. It is impossible to argue against the fact that Vladimir Monomakh acted well when he fought and overcame the Polovtsians, and the General also acted well when he annihilated the Bashi-Bazouks.

LADY – Then you agree with them?

POLITICIAN – I agree with that which I have the honor of stating before you now: that *in the given circumstances* both Monomakh and the General acted just as they should have acted. But how are we to evaluate those circumstances? Are we to justify the perpetuation of war and militarism?

PRINCE – This is just what I was about to say.

LADY – Then you agree with the Prince?

POLITICIAN – If you will allow me to explain my view of the subject, you will see with whom and with what I agree. My view is only a logical conclusion drawn from actual life and the facts of history. How can one argue against the historical importance of war when it is the main, if not the only, instrument by which the State has been created and gradually consolidated? Show me a single State which was founded and made secure otherwise than by war.

LADY – What about North America, the United States?

POLITICIAN – I thank you for an excellent example. I am, however, speaking of the creation of a *State*. The United States, as a European *colony*, was, of course, founded not by war but by exploration, just as all other colonies were. But the moment this colony wished to become a State, it had to earn its political independence by means of a long war.

PRINCE – From the fact that the State has been created by war, which is, I agree, indisputable, you seem to conclude that war is all-important. In my opinion, however, the only conclusion which can be drawn from this fact is the unimportance of the State for those people who no longer believe in the worship of violence.

POLITICIAN – Why suddenly "the worship of violence"? What for? Try to establish a stable human community outside the compulsory forms of the State, or try to reject in practice everything that takes its life from the State. Only when you can do that will you be able to speak legitimately of the unimportance of the State. But until you do so, the State, and everything for which you and I are indebted to it, will remain a colossal fact, while your attacks against it remain but empty words. I repeat that the supreme historical importance of war, as the principal condition in the creation of a State, is beyond any doubt. But I ask you: Is it not right to regard this great task of creating States as already completed in its broad outlines? As to the details, these can be settled without having recourse to such an heroic instrument as war. In ancient times and during the Middle Ages, when the world of European culture was merely an island in the midst of an ocean of more or less barbarous tribes, the military system was necessitated by the very instinct of self-preservation. It was at that time necessary to be always ready to repel any hordes that suddenly swooped down from an unsuspected quarter to trample the feeble growth of civilization. At present it is only the non-European elements that can be described as islands, while European culture has become the ocean which is gradually washing these islands away. Our scientists, explorers, and missionaries have searched the whole earth without finding anything that is likely to menace seriously our civilized world. Wild tribes are successfully destroying themselves and are dying out, while militant barbarians, like the Turks and Japanese, are being civilized and are losing their liking for warfare. In the meanwhile, the process of uniting the European nations in the common bond of civilized life —

LADY (*in a whisper*) – Monte Carlo . . .

POLITICIAN – in the common bond of civilized life has grown to such an extent that war amongst these nations would really be something in the nature of fratricide, which could not be excused on any grounds now that peaceful settlement of international disputes has become possible. It would be as fantastic in our time to solve such disputes by war as it would be to travel from St. Petersburg to Marseilles in a sailing boat or in a coach driven by a troika. I quite agree, of course, that "A lonely sail is looming white in the blue mist of the sea" or "See the troika flitting wild"[3] sounds vastly more poetic than the screeching of steam engines or cries of "*En voiture, messieurs!*" In the same way I am prepared to admit the aesthetic superiority of the "bristling steel of lances" and of "with swinging step in shining array the army is marching along" over diplomatic portfolios and the cloth-covered tables of congresses of peace. But the serious attitude toward this vital question must obviously be entirely independent of the aesthetic appreciation of the beauty which belongs not to real war (this, I can assure you, has very little of the beautiful) but to its reflection in the imaginations of the poet and the artist. Well, then, once it has been understood by everybody that

[3] Quotations from popular poems by Lermontov and Pushkin — Translator.

war, however interesting for poets and painters (these, of course, could be well satisfied with past wars), is unprofitable now — for it is too costly and risky a means of achieving ends which can be achieved at much less cost and in a more certain way by other methods — *then it follows that the military period of history is over.* I am speaking, of course, *en grand.* The immediate disarmament of nations is out of the question. But I do firmly believe that neither ourselves nor our children will ever see a great war — a real European war — and that our grandchildren will learn only of little wars — somewhere in Asia or Africa — and of past wars from historical works.

So here is my answer with regard to Vladimir Monomakh. When it became necessary to protect the future of the newly born Russian State, first from the Polovtsians, then from the Tartars, and so on, war was a most necessary and important enterprise. The same, with certain limitations, may be applied to the period of Peter the Great, when it was necessary to ensure the future of Russia as a *European* power. But since then war's importance has become ever more disputable, and today, as I have already said, the military period of history is over in Russia, just as it is over everywhere else. What I have said about our fatherland can be applied, of course, *mutatis mutandis,* to the other European countries. In every one of them war was, in the past, the main and inevitable means of defending and strengthening the existence of the State and the nation. But now, this object having been attained, war has everywhere lost its *raison d'être*

I may say, parenthetically, that I am puzzled to find some modern philosophers discussing the "rational basis of war" as an issue independent of any particular time and place. Has war any rational basis? *C'est selon.* Yesterday it probably had a rational basis everywhere; today it has a rational basis only somewhere in Africa and Central Asia, where savagery still obtains. Tomorrow it will be justified nowhere. It is remarkable that with the loss of its rational basis war is, though slowly, losing its mystical halo. This can be seen even in a nation so backward in the mass as our own. Judge for yourself: the other day the General triumphantly pointed out the fact that all our saints are either monks or soldiers. But to what historical period does all this military holiness or holy militarism actually belong? Does it not belong to that very long period during which war was in reality the most necessary, saving, and (if you will) most holy enterprise? Our warrior saints were all princes of the Kiev and Mongolian periods, but I fail to recollect any lieutenant generals among them. What is the meaning of it all? You have two famous warriors having exactly the same personal rights to saintship, but the honor is granted to one and refused to the other. Why is that so? Tell me why Alexander Nevsky, who overthrew the Livonians and Swedes in the thirteenth century, is a saint, whereas Alexander Suvorov, who overcame the Turks and the French in the eighteenth century, is not.[4] You cannot reproach Suvorov with anything incompatible with holiness. He was sincerely pious, used to sing publicly in the church choir and read the Bible from the lectern, led an irreproachable life, was not even any woman's lover, while his role as one of "God's fools" makes no obstacle to, but rather supplies, a further argument for his being canonized. The sole difference is that Alexander Nevsky fought for the national and political future of his country, which,

---

[4] Alexander Nevsky (1220–1263) was the Novrogorodian prince who successfully led his forces against the Swedes and Germans. The Order (or Medal) of Alexander Nevksy is awarded for bravery and valor. Count Alexander Vasilyevich Suvorov (1730–1800) brilliantly commanded the Russian armies in the Russo-Turkish war of 1787–91 and was created Count Rymnitsky by Catherine II and a Count of the Reich by the Holy Roman Emperor. In 1799 he expelled the French from Italy and was appointed generalissimo of the Russian forces. He died, however, in disgrace — Editor.

half battered-down from the East, could scarcely survive another battering from the West. The people grasped intuitively the vital importance of the situation and gave the Prince the highest reward they could possibly bestow upon him by canonizing him. Whereas the achievements of Suvorov, though greatly superior in the military sense, particularly his Hannibalian passage of the Alps, did not respond to any pressing need; he was not obliged to save Russia, and so, you see, he has forever remained merely a military celebrity.

LADY – But the leaders of the Russian army in 1812 were saving Russia from Napoleon — why were they not canonized?

POLITICIAN – "Saving Russia from Napoleon" is merely patriotic rhetoric. Napoleon could not have swallowed us up, nor did he intend to. The fact that we finally got the upper hand certainly revealed our power as a nation and a State and helped to awaken our national consciousness. But I can never admit that the war of 1812 was caused by any pressing necessity. We could very well have come to terms with Napoleon. It is true that we could not oppose him without taking some risks, risks that proved lucky for us; and it is true that the war was brought to an end in a way that greatly flattered our national self-esteem. Yet that war's subsequent effects could hardly be regarded as really useful. If I see two athletes without any conceivable reason suddenly falling upon each other and one worsting the other, neither suffering any harm to his health, I might perhaps say of the victor, "He is a good sport!" But the need of just this particular sportsmanship and of no other would remain for me very obscure. The fame of 1812, the national virtues revealed at that time, remain with us, whatever the causes of the war may have been.

The sacred truth of 1812
Was still alive in people's eyes.

This is very good for poetry: "the sacred truth!" But I turn to what came of that truth, and I find on the one side the archimandrite Photius, Magnitsky, Arakcheyev, and on the other side the Decembrist conspiracy and, *en somme*, that thirty years' long regime of belated militarism, which eventually brought us to the debacle of the Crimean War. [5]

LADY – And what about Pushkin?

POLITICIAN – Pushkin? Why Pushkin?

LADY – I recently read in the papers that the national poetry of Pushkin owed its inspiration to the military glories of 1812.

MR. Z. – And not without some special participation of artillery, as the poet's name indicates. [6]

POLITICIAN – Yes; perhaps that is really how it is. But to continue my argument. As years roll on the uselessness of our wars becomes more and more clear. The Crimean War is regarded in Russia as very important, as it is generally believed that the liberation of the serfs and all the other reforms of Alexander II were due to its failure. Even supposing this was so, the beneficial effects of an unsuccessful war, effects that were beneficial only because the war was unsuccessful, cannot, of course, serve as an apology for war in general. If I, without any satisfactory reason, try jumping off the balcony and end up putting my arm out of joint, and later on this dislocation prevents me

[5] Three anti-Enlightenment figures: Archimandrite Photius was a young, ascetic, influential Russian monk who, in the 1820's, as unofficial adviser to Tsar Alexander I, was a spokesperson for the xenophobic Church hierarchy; Michael Leontyevich Magnitsky (1778–1885), a politican and reformer, edited the reactionary journal *Raduga*; Count Alexey Andreyevich Arakcheyev (1769–1834), soldier and statesman, was a stern and conservative adviser to Tsar Paul I and Tsar Alexander I — during the latter's frequent absences abroad he virtually ruled Russia. The Decembrist conspiracy arose against Tsar Nicholas I on his accession to the Russian throne in December, 1825 — Translator.

[6] "Pushkin" — of the "pushka" — of the cannon — Translator.

from signing a ruinous promissory note, I shall be glad that
events turned out the way they did; but I will not say that
it is generally recommended to jump off balconies rather
than walking down by the stairs. You will agree that if the
head is not hurt there is no need to hurt the arm to escape
signing a ruinous agreement; one and the same good sense
will save one from a foolish leap from a balcony and a
foolish signature. I believe that even if there had been no
Crimean War the reforms of Alexander II would most
probably have been carried out, and perhaps in a more
secure and far-reaching way. But I am not going to prove
this now; we must see that we do not depart from our
subject. The point is that political acts cannot be rated by
their indirect and unforeseen consequences. And as to the
Crimean War, which began with the advance of our army
to the Danube in 1853, it had no reasonable justification. I
cannot call sensible a policy that one day saves Turkey from
a smashing defeat at the hands of Mehmet Ali[7], the Pasha
of Egypt (and thus prevents the division of the Moslem
world around two centers, Istanbul and Cairo — a division
which, it seems to me, would not have done us much
harm), and that next day tries to destroy this same spared
and reinforced Turkey, with the risk of running against the
whole of the European coalition. This is not policy, but a
sort of Quixotism. I would apply the same name — if the
General will forgive me this — also to our last Turkish war.

LADY – And the Bashi-Bazouks in Armenia? Didn't you
approve of the General for annihilating them?

POLITICIAN – Forgive me, but I maintain that, at the
present time, war has become *useless*, and the story told by

[7] Mehmet Ali (1769–1849) fought against Napoleon at Abukir (1799);
made Pasha by Sheiks of Cairo (1805); left without a rival in Egypt by
massacre of Mamelukes (1811); waged war against Wahabis (1811–18);
subdued Nubia and Kardofan (1823); granted possession of Crete (1830);
defeated Turks at Nizib (1839), but deprived by Great Powers of spoils of
victory; retired to hereditary viceroyalty of Egypt (1841) — Editor.

the General the other day bears this out particularly well. I quite understand that anybody whose military duty made him an active participant in the war, and who happened to come across irregular Turkish troops inflicting terrible barbarities upon the peaceful population — I say that anyone, that everyone (*looking at the Prince*) free from preconceived "absolute principles," would be obliged by sentiment and by duty alike to exterminate those Bashi-Bazouks without mercy, as the General did, and not worry, as the Prince would have, about their moral regeneration. But, I ask, in the first place, who was the real cause of all this wretched business? And, in the second place, what has been achieved by the military intervention? To the first question I can answer in all honor only by pointing to that bad militant policy which irritated the Turks by inflaming the passions and supporting the pretensions of the Christian populations. It was only when Bulgaria began to swarm with revolutionary committees and the Turks became alarmed at foreign interference and the fall of their State that the Turks began to slaughter the Bulgarians. The same thing also happened in Armenia. As to the second question, what has come out of it? The answer supplied by recent events is so striking that nobody can help noticing it. Judge for yourself: in 1877 our General destroys a few thousand Bashi-Bazouks and by this *probably* saves a few hundred Armenians. In 1895, in the very same place, very much the same Bashi-Bazouks slaughter not hundreds but thousands, perhaps even tens of thousands, of the population. If various correspondents can be trusted (though I myself would not advise anyone to trust them), the number of people massacred was nearly half a million. That may very well be an exaggeration. But there can be little doubt that these later Armenian massacres were carried out on a much larger scale than the prior Bulgarian ones. There you have the beneficent results of our patriotic and philanthropic war.

GENERAL – Can you understand this? First it is bad policy

that is to blame, then it is the patriotic war. One might believe that Prince Gorchakov and M. Giers were soldiers, [8] or that Disraeli and Bismarck were Russian patriots and philanthropists.

POLITICIAN – Is my statement really not clear enough? I have in mind the perfectly indisputable — neither abstract nor ideal, but rather wholly real and pragmatic — connection between the war of 1877, which was brought about by our bad policy, and the recent massacres of Christians in Armenia. You probably know, and, if you don't, you will profit by learning it, that after 1878 Turkey, who could see her future prospects in Europe in terms of the San Stefano agreement, resolved at all events to secure her position in Asia. First of all, she obtained an English guarantee of support at the Berlin Congress. Then, rightly following the maxim "count on England but don't slip up," the Turkish government set about reestablishing and reinforcing the irregular armies in Armenia, more or less those very "devils" the General dealt with. This proved a very sound policy; only fifteen years passed after Disraeli had, in exchange for Cyprus, guaranteed Turkey her Asiatic dominions, when English policy, in view of changed circumstances, became anti-Turkish and Armeniophile, while English agitators appeared in Armenia as Slavophile agitators had earlier in Bulgaria. At that moment, those familiar to the General as "devils" found themselves "the men of the hour," and with the most polished manners helped themselves to the largest portion of Christian meat that had ever reached their teeth.

GENERAL – This is disgusting! Why should the war be blamed for this? Good Heavens! If only the wise statesmen

[8] Alexander Mikhailovich Gorchakov (1798–1883), one of the most noteworthy diplomats of 19th century Europe; Nicholas Karlovich Giers (1820–1895), a politician, married into the family of prince Gorchakov, whom he succeeded — Editor.

had finished their business in 1878 as well as the soldiers did theirs. If they had, you may be sure there would have been not even a mention of any reestablishment or reinforcement of irregular armies in Armenia. Consequently, there would have been no massacres.

POLITICIAN – In other words, you mean to say that the Turkish Empire ought to have been totally destroyed?

GENERAL – Emphatically I do. I am sincerely fond of the Turks, and have much esteem for them. They are a fine people, especially when compared with all these nondescript Ethiopians. Yet I verily believe that it is time for us to put an end to this Turkish Empire.

POLITICIAN – I should have nothing to say against this, if those Ethiopians of yours would be able to establish in its place some sort of Ethiopian Empire of their own. But, up to the present, they can only fight each other, and a Turkish Government is as much necessary for them as the presence of Turkish troops is necessary in Jerusalem for preserving the peace and well-being of the various Christian denominations there.

LADY – Indeed! I have always suspected that you would not object to handing over the Lord's sepulcher to the Turks forever.

POLITICIAN – And you, of course, think that this would be because of my atheism or indifference, don't you? As a matter of fact, however, my wish to see the Turks in Jerusalem is the reflection of a faint but inextinguishable spark of religious sentiment which I still preserve from my childhood. I know positively that the moment the Turkish soldiers are withdrawn from the streets of Jerusalem all the Christians in the city will massacre each other, after having destroyed all the Christian shrines. If you doubt my impressions and conclusions, just ask any pilgrims whom you may trust, or, what is even better, go and see for yourself.

LADY – Go to Jerusalem? Oh no! What could I see there? . . . No. I would be afraid to.

POLITICIAN – Well, that only bears out my statement.

LADY – I cannot understand this at all. You argue with the General, and yet you both extol the Turks.

POLITICIAN – The General values them apparently as brave soldiers, and I value them as the guardians of peace and order in the East.

LADY – Fine peace and order, indeed, when some tens of thousands of people are suddenly and mercilessly slaughtered. Personally, I would prefer disorder.

POLITICIAN – As I have already had the honor of stating, the massacres were caused by the revolutionary agitation. Why should you then demand from the Turks a higher degree of Christian meekness and forbearance than is ever demanded from any other nation, not excepting a Christian one? Can you name me a country where an armed insurrection has ever been quelled without recourse to harsh and unjust measures? In the case before us, in the first place, the instigators of the massacres were not the Turks. In the second place, Turks proper took hardly any part in them, acting in most cases through the General's "devils." And in the third place, I am prepared to admit that the Turkish government, by letting loose these "devils," overdid the thing; as Ivan IV overdid it when he drowned ten thousand peaceful inhabitants of Novgorod; or as the commissioners of the French Convention overdid it by their *noyades* and *fusillades*; or lastly, as the English overdid it in India when they quelled the insurrection of 1857. And yet there can be little doubt that should these various Ethiopians be left alone, there would be many more massacres than under the Turks.

GENERAL – Who told you I want to put these Ethiopians in the place of Turkey? Surely, the thing is very simple: we should take Constantinople, we should take Jerusalem, and in the place of the Turkish Empire we should form a few Russian military provinces, like Samarkand or Ashkhabad.

As to the Turks, they, after they had laid down their arms, should in every way be satisfied and pleased, in religion as much as in everything else.

POLITICIAN – I trust you are not serious now, or I shall be obliged to doubt . . . your patriotism. Don't you see that, if we started a war with such radical ends in view, this would certainly revive a European coalition against us, which our Ethiopians, liberated or promised liberation, would ultimately join? These latter understand very well that under Russian power they would not be so free to express "their national physiognomy," as the Bulgarians say. And the end of it all would be that, instead of destroying the Turkish Empire, we should have a repetition *en grand* of the Sebastopol debacle. No, though we have indulged in bad politics sufficiently often, I am sure that we shall never see such madness as a new war with Turkey. If we do, then every patriot must exclaim with despair about Russia: *Quem Deus vult perdere, prius dementat.*

LADY – What does that mean?

POLITICIAN – It means: Whom God would destroy, He first drives mad.

LADY – I am glad history is not made according to your argument. You are, I suppose, as much in favor of Austria as of Turkey?

POLITICIAN – I need not enlarge upon this, as people more competent than myself — the national leaders of Bohemia, for example — have declared long ago: "If there were no Austria, Austria would have to be invented." The recent brawls in the Vienna Parliament supply the best possible illustration of this maxim, and are a vision in miniature of what must happen in these countries should the Hapsburg Empire disappear.

LADY – And what is your opinion about the Franco-Russian Alliance? You always seem to have some reservations about it.

POLITICIAN – Neither do I propose to go into the details of this delicate question just now. Speaking generally, I can say the rapprochement with such a progressive and rich nation as France is beneficial to us. On the other hand, this alliance is, of course, an alliance of peace and precaution. This is, at any rate, the meaning which is put on it in the high circles where it was concluded and is still supported.

MR. Z. – As to the benefits of rapprochement between two nations for the development of their morals and culture, this is a complicated matter, which to me seems very obscure. But looking at it from the political point of view, don't you think that by joining one of the two hostile camps on the European continent we lose the advantage of our free position as neutral judge or arbiter between them? Don't we lose our impartiality? By joining one side, and thereby balancing the powers of both groups, don't we create the possibility of an armed conflict between them? It is, for instance, clear that France alone could not fight against the Triple Alliance, whereas with the help of Russia she could certainly do so.

POLITICIAN – Your considerations would be quite correct if anyone had any wish to begin a European war. But I can assure you that nobody has such a wish. At any rate, it is much easier for Russia to prevent France from leaving the path of peace than it would be for France to lure Russia into the path of war. War is undesirable, in fact, to both of them. Here is the most reassuring thing — not only are modern nations averse to waging war but, more importantly, they *are beginning to forget how to do so.* Take, for example, the latest conflict, the Spanish-American war. Was this a war? I ask you: Was it really a war? It was mere dolls' play; a ruckus between a street brawler and a constable! "After a long and furious fight the enemy retreated, having lost two men, one killed and one wounded. We sustained no losses." Or: "The whole of the enemy's squadron, after a desperate struggle with our cruiser *Sufficent Capital*, surrendered unconditionally. No losses either dead or wounded were sustained on either side." There you have the whole war. I am surprised that everyone seems to be so little surprised at this new character of war — its bloodlessness, so to speak. The metamorphosis has been taking place before our very eyes, as we all can remember the sort of bulletins published in 1870 and in 1877.

GENERAL – Wait a little with your surprise until two really military nations come into collision. You will see then what sort of bulletins are issued!

POLITICIAN – I am not so sure. How long is it since Spain was a first-class military nation? Thank God, the past cannot return. It appears to me that just as in the body useless organs become atrophied, so it is in humanity: the fighting qualities have lost their usefulness, and so they disappear. Should they suddenly reappear, I should be as startled as if a bat had suddenly acquired eagle eyes or human beings again found themselves with tails.

LADY – But why, then, did you yourself praise the Turkish soldiers?

POLITICIAN – I praised them as guardians of peace within the State. In this sense military power or, as it is called, "the mailed fist," *manus militaris*, will for a long time still be necessary for humanity. But this does not contradict the fact that militancy in the sense of the disposition and ability to wage international wars, this national *pugnacity*, so to speak, must entirely disappear and is already disappearing before our eyes, degenerating into that bloodless though not altogether harmless form which is exemplified in parliamentary squabbles. The disposition to such displays will apparently remain as long as there are conflicting parties and opinions, and so in order to check them the *manus militaris* will necessarily remain in the State, even at the time when external wars, that is, wars between nations or states, will long have become merely things of the historical past.

General – That is to say, you liken the police to the coccyx, which still exists in man, although only the Kievan witches are credited with proper tails! How witty! But aren't you just a little too ready with your comparison? Your conclusion is that just because some nation or other degenerates, becomes flabby, and can no longer fight, therefore the military virtues are decadent or lost all the world over! It is possible that under the introduction of "legislative measures" and "systems" even Russian soldiers may soften to jelly! Heaven preserve us!

Lady (*to the Politician*) – You have not yet explained how, war being excepted, such questions as, for instance, the Eastern Question should be solved. However wicked the Christian nations in the East may be, if they feel a desire to be independent at any cost, the Turks will for this reason slaughter them. Surely you don't suggest that we should look on with folded arms? Supposing that your criticisms of past wars are really sound, I shall ask, like the Prince, though in a different sense: "What are we to do now, should massacres begin again somewhere?"

Politician – Before they do begin, we must quietly exercise our judgment, and instead of a bad policy follow a good one, even though it be German; that is to say, we must not irritate the Turks, and we must not shout when in our cups about raising the Cross on the mosques. We must in a peaceful and friendly manner civilize Turkey for our mutual benefit: for our benefit, as much as for Turkey's. It depends entirely on us to make the Turks understand as rapidly as possible that slaughtering inhabitants in one's own country is not only a bad thing in itself, but above all that it has no use and yields no profit.

Mr. Z. – These suggestions of yours involve railway concessions and all sorts of trade and commercial interests in which the Germans, I am sure, will forestall us, and

competition with them in this direction would be a hopeless task. [9]

POLITICIAN – But why should we compete? If somebody
does hard work for me, I shall be only too glad and
thankful. If, however, this makes me angry with him, so
that I ask: "Why did he do it and not I?" I am acting in a
way which would be unworthy of a respectable person.
Similarly, it would be unworthy of such a nation as Russia
to imitate the dog in the manger which, lying on the hay,
neither eats nor lets others eat. If others, using their own
means, can do more quickly and better the good we also
desire, then so much the more profitable is it for us. I ask
you: Were not all our wars with Turkey during the nineteenth century waged only for the sake of safeguarding the
human rights of the Turkish Christians? Now, what if the
Germans achieve the same object in a sure, though peaceful, way by *civilizing* Turkey? It is clear that had they been
as firmly established in Asia Minor in 1895 as the English
are in Egypt, we should not have to discuss Armenian
massacres any longer.

LADY – You have already suggested that it is necessary to
make an end of Turkey. But you are, for some unknown
reason, anxious to see her eaten up by the Germans.

POLITICIAN – It is just because the German policy has no
desire to swallow such indigestible articles that I called it
wise. Its object is more subtle: it is to bring Turkey into the
company of the civilized nations, to help the Turks in
educating themselves and making themselves capable of
undertaking a just and humane control over nations which,
owing to their mutual savage hostility, are unable to direct
their own affairs peacefully.

LADY – What fairy tales are these? Who will ever think it

[9] These words, written by me in October 1899, were fully borne out in
a month's time by the announced German-Turkish convention concerning
Asia Minor and the Baghdad railway — Author.

possible to surrender a Christian people to the Turks for eternal control? I like the Turks myself for many things, but still they are barbarians, and their last word will always be violence. A European culture will only make them worse.

POLITICIAN – Exactly the same could be said about Russia at the time of Peter the Great, and even much later. We remember "Turkish barbarities," but how long has it been in Russia and in other countries as well since "Turkish barbarities" became unknown? "The poor unhappy Christians groaning under the Moslem yoke!" What about those who groaned under the yoke of our wicked landlords — were they Christians or pagans? Or what about the soldiers who groaned under the punishment of the rod? The only just and reasonable answer to these groans of the Russian peasants was the abolition of serfdom and of the rod — not the destruction of the Russian Empire. Why, then, must the answer to the Bulgarian and Armenian groans be of necessity the destruction of the State in which these groans are heard?

LADY – It is one thing when disgusting things that can be easily reformed occur in a Christian state. It is another thing when a Christian people are being oppressed by a non-Christian people.

POLITICIAN – The impossibility of reforming Turkey is merely a rooted prejudice which the Germans are disproving before our eyes, just as they earlier helped to destroy the prejudice of the inborn savagery of the Russian people. As to your distinction between "Christians" and "non-Christians," you will do well to remember that, for the *victims* of barbarities, this question is lacking in interest. If anybody strips off my skin, I shall surely not ask him: "What is your religion, sir?" Neither shall I be at all consoled if I find out that the people torturing me are not only extremely unpleasant and disturbing to me, but on the top of this, being Christians themselves, are exceedingly abhorrent to their own God who sees his commands openly defied. Speaking objectively, it cannot be denied that the "Christianity" of Ivan the Terrible, or Saltykova, or Arakcheyev [10] is not in any sense an advantage but, rather, so utterly base that it is impossible to meet with its like in other religions. Yesterday the General was describing the dastardly deeds of the savage Kurds, and among other things he mentioned their devil worship. It is certainly very wicked to roast babies or grown-up people over a slow fire — I am quite prepared to call such acts devilish. It is a well-known fact, however, that Ivan the Terrible was particularly fond of this very roasting of human beings on a slow fire. He would even keep the fire underneath well poked! And yet he was not a savage or a devil worshipper but, rather, a man of keen intellect, and, for the age in which he lived, a man of wide learning. At the same time, he was also a theologian firmly attached to orthodoxy. But we need not probe so far into the remote past. Take the Bulgarian Stambulov and the Serbian Milan [11] — are they Turks, or are they representatives of the so-called Christian nations? What is this "Christianity" of yours if not an empty title which carries with it no guarantee of anything?

LADY – One would think it is the Prince expounding his faith. How strange!

POLITICIAN – When obvious truth is concerned, I am willing to be at one not only with our esteemed Prince but even with Balaam's ass!

[10] The Moscow landlady of the middle of the eighteenth century, Saltykova, nicknamed Saltychikha, the favorite of Alexander I, and General Arakcheyev have become famous in Russia for the monstrous way in which they treated those under their power — Translator.

[11] Stefan Stambulov (1855–1895), Bulgarian statesman, president of the *Sobranje* (1885–86), premier (1887–94), assassinated; Milan Obrenovic (1854–1901), Prince (1862–82) and King (1882–89) of Serbia. Forced by popular pan-Slavic sentiment to declare war against Turkey, he was defeated but, owing to Russia's victory over Turkey and Austrian support, gained Serbian independence — Editor.

MR. Z. – But if my memory does not fail me, your Excellency has kindly agreed to take the leading part in today's discussion — not with the idea of arguing about Christianity or the animals of the Bible. I can hear ringing in my ears your *soulful prayer*: "Only as little religion as possible! For God's sake, as little religion as you can help!" Remembering this, may it please your Excellency to return to the subject of our discussion and to explain one little thing that is puzzling me. It is this. As you have rightly stated, our object must be not the destruction of the Turkish Empire but the work of its civilization. On the other hand, as you also admitted on quite reasonable grounds, the advancement of Turkey along the path of culture will be, and is now, much better carried on by the Germans than it could ever be carried on by us. Now, if both these statements are correct, will you be good enough to tell me what objective, in your opinion, remains for Russia — what special and solely Russian policy can we have in the Eastern question?

POLITICIAN – A special policy for Russia? Why, it is clear that no such policy can exist. As you understand it, the *special* Russian policy is obviously one which would be set up and pursued by Russia independently of and against the plans of all the other European nations. But I must tell you that, as a matter of fact, no such policy has ever been pursued. We have deviated sometimes toward such a policy, as, for instance, in the fifties and later on in the seventies; but those regrettable deviations, giving examples of what I may call *bad* policy, have instantly brought their own reward in the shape of reverses of greater or smaller significance. Generally speaking, it is quite impossible to regard Russian policy in the Eastern question as independent or isolated. The object of Russia's policy from the sixteenth century almost to the end of the eighteenth century was to defend the civilized world from the threatened invasion of the Turks, working in cooperation with Poland and Austria. As in that defense we were obliged to act conjointly with the Poles, the Austrians, and the Republic of Venice, though free from any formal alliances, it is evident that that policy was a common and not an independent one. In the nineteenth century, and it will be much more so in the twentieth century, our policy's cooperative character has remained and must remain the same as before, though naturally its aim and means have of necessity changed. The problem now is not to defend Europe from Turkish barbarism, but to make the Turks themselves more European. The old aim required military means; today the means must be peaceful. In both cases, however, our task remains the same: As formerly the European nations were bound in solidarity by the interests of military defense, so today they are bound in solidarity by the interests of spreading civilization.

GENERAL – And yet the old military solidarity did not prevent Richelieu and Louis XIV from entering into alliances with Turkey against the Hapsburgs.

POLITICIAN – Precisely the bad Bourbon policy which, along with their senseless internal politics, duly received its just reward from history.

LADY – You call this history? It used to be called regicide, if I am not mistaken.

POLITICIAN (*to Lady*) – The words matter little. What remains is the fact that no political mistake passes off without retribution. Those inclined to do so may see in this something mystical. But I find as little of what is mystical in this case as I would were I, in my present age and position, to start drinking champagne glass after glass as if I were again a young man, instead of continuing to satisfy myself with my current milk diet. I would undoubtedly become ill, and were I too persistent in my champagne *ancien régime*, I should at last die off, as the Bourbons did.

LADY – You cannot dispute that your *milk diet* policy becomes, in the end, as exceedingly tedious as any Bourbon policy.

POLITICIAN (*offended*) – If I had not been interrupted, I should have long ago exhausted my subject and given place to someone more entertaining.

LADY – Please don't take offense. I was merely joking. On the contrary, I think you have been very witty . . . for your age and position.

POLITICIAN – So I say that we are at one with the rest of Europe in the object of reforming Turkey on the lines of culture, and we have not at present, nor can we ever have, any special independent policy. It must, however, be added that on account of our comparative backwardness in social development, and in industry and trade, the share of Russia in this common cause of civilizing the Turkish Empire cannot be very great at present. The foremost importance that our country had as a military State cannot, of course, be retained by us now. Predominance is not acquired for nothing; it must be earned. We earned our military importance not by mere bluff but by actual wars and victories. In the same way, our importance in the work of civilization must be earned by actual labor and successes in peaceful callings. As the Turks had to fall back before our military victories, they will now retire before those who prove themselves to be strongest in the sphere of peaceful progress. What is there left for us to do, in that case? You will find hardly anywhere today the blatant insanity that believes that the mere ideal of the imaginary raising of the Cross on St. Sophia is a more powerful force in itself than is the actual superiority of the Germans.

GENERAL – The only thing is that this Cross must not be imaginary.

POLITICIAN – But who will materialize it for you? So long as you have not found the means to do so, the only thing demanded by our national ambition — within the reasonable limits in which this feeling can be recognized at all — is to double our efforts so that, as quickly as possible, we may come into line with other nations in the areas in which we now lag behind. By doing this, we should gain the time and effort wasted on various Slav committees and similar poisonous nonsense. Besides, though as yet we may be powerless in Turkey, we are nevertheless already capable of playing a leading part in civilizing Central Asia, and particularly the Far East, whither, it appears, the history of the world is transferring its center of gravity. Owing to her geographical situation, and other advantageous conditions, Russia can do more there than any other nation except, of course, England. It follows, then, that the object of our policy in this respect must be to secure a permanent and amiable understanding with England, so that our cooperation with her in the work of civilization may never change into a senseless hostility and unworthy competition.

MR. Z. – Unfortunately, some such transformation always comes about, with single individuals as much as with nations, as if it were a part of their destiny.

POLITICIAN – It is true, that does happen. On the other hand, I don't know of a single case in the life of human beings, or in the life of nations, in which hostility and envy displayed toward their coadjutors in a common cause has ever helped to make any one of them stronger, richer, and happier. This universal experience, to which not a single exception may be found, is made use of by intelligent people. And I believe that a nation as intelligent as Russia will not fail to make use of it either. Quarrel with the English in the Far East? Why, this would be the most utter madness, not to speak of the indecency of indulging in domestic quarrels before strangers. Or do you perhaps think that we are more closely related to the yellow-faced Chinese than to the compatriots of Shakespeare and Byron?

MR. Z. – This is a delicate question.

POLITICIAN – Then we'll leave it alone for a time. Here is

something else to consider. From what I have said, you will understand that I recognize only two legitimate objectives for Russian policy: first, the maintenance of peace in Europe (for any European war at the present stage of historical evolution would amount to an insane and criminal internecine struggle); and second, the civilizing of the barbarian nations within the sphere of our influence. Now, if you accept my point of view, you will see that these two objectives, apart from the intrinsic value that each has separately, depend upon each other for their very existence. It is obvious, then, that, if we really do all we can to give the benefits of civilization to the barbarian countries — work all Europe is equally interested in — we thereby draw together the bonds of solidarity between ourselves and other nations; and that, while thus consolidating European unity, we, by this very fact, strengthen our influence among the barbarous nations, as we leave them no hope of successful resistance. Don't you think that, if the yellow race knew that all Europe were behind Russia, we could do in Asia anything we wished? If, however, China saw that Europe were not behind Russia, but against her, it would not hesitate even to attack our frontiers, and we should have to defend ourselves on two fronts along a line ten thousand versts long. I do not believe in the "Yellow Peril," because I do not admit the possibility of a European war. But, *given the latter*, we should then have to fear even the Mongolians.

GENERAL – To you, a European war or a Mongolian invasion seems to be absolutely out of the range of possibility. But, I must confess, I have very little faith in your "solidarity of the European nations" and your coming "peace of the world." Somehow, it seems both highly unnatural and exceedingly unlikely. Remember the old Christmas hymn, "Peace on earth and goodwill towards men?" Peace will reign on the earth only when goodwill is established. But where is this goodwill now? Have you ever seen it? To be quite frank, both you and I feel a real and sincere goodwill only to one European power — the principality of Monaco. Inviolable, also, is our peace with it. But to regard the Germans or the English as *our own* family, to feel that their benefit is our benefit, their pleasure is our pleasure — such a "solidarity," as you call it, with the European nations, I am sure, we shall never have.

POLITICIAN – Why "we shall never have" when it is already with us, when it is in the very nature of things? We are at one with the European powers for the simple reason that we are Europeans ourselves. This has been *un fait accompli* since the eighteenth century, and neither the total lack of culture among the Russian masses nor the unfortunate chimeras of the Slavophiles will ever be able to alter it.

GENERAL – But do the Europeans agree among themselves? The French with the Germans, for instance; the English with both of these? It is rumored that even the Swedes and the Norwegians have somewhere lost their solidarity!

POLITICIAN – What a forceful argument! But what a pity that all its force rests on a defective basis — on the total neglect of the historical situation. Let me ask you a question: Would Moscow have been at one with Novgorod at the time of Ivan III or Ivan the Terrible? Will you, on the strength of this, deny the solidarity of the Moscow and Novgorod provinces in the common interests of the State?

GENERAL – No, not at all. But this I will say: Let us wait a little before declaring ourselves Europeans — at least until that historic moment when all the European nations are as firmly bound together as are our provinces in the Russian State. Surely, you will not advise us to tear ourselves to pieces working for solidarity with all other Europeans when they themselves are at daggers drawn?

POLITICIAN – "At daggers drawn," you say! But you need not worry. You will be saved from the necessity of tearing yourself to pieces between Norway and Sweden and between France and Germany for the simple reason that these states will never come to a rupture. At present, this seems obvious. Only in Russia can you find a small group of adventurers who back France against Germany. They ought to be shut up in prison. Let them preach their war against Germany there and develop their patriotism.

LADY – It would really be a very good thing if it were possible to put in prison all those who foment strife among nations. But I think you are wrong.

POLITICIAN – Of course, what I have said must be taken with a grain of salt. It is quite true that, on the surface, Europe has not yet become consolidated into a whole. But I still stand by my historical analogy. For instance, in our country in the sixteenth century, separation among various provinces, though still present, was at its last gasp, while the unity of the State had long ago ceased to be a dream and was actually shaping itself into definite forms. So likewise in modern Europe, though national antagonism still exists, particularly among the ignorant masses and half-educated politicians, it is not strong enough to transform itself into any considerable action: that it will not go so far as to lead to a European war I am positively certain. As to the goodwill of which you are speaking, General, to tell you the truth, I fail to see it, not only among different nations but within any nation itself, or even within single families. If you do meet it occasionally, it does not go further than the first generation. What conclusion can be drawn from this? Certainly not a reason for internecine wars and fratricide. Similarly, in international relations: The French and Germans may dislike each other if they wish, but let them abstain from actual fighting. I am sure that there won't be any.

MR. Z. – This is very probable. But even regarding Europe as a single whole, we cannot conclude from this that we ourselves are Europeans. You know there is an opinion which has become fairly popular during the last twenty years that Europe, that is, the combination of all the German and Latin nations, is really a distinct type characterized by political unanimity and by common culture and history; it is further maintained that we Russians do not belong to this group but constitute a separate Greco-Slavonic type.

POLITICIAN – I have heard of this variety of Slavophilism and have even had occasion to speak with some of those holding this view. There is one thing I have noticed about this theory, however, and it seems to me to give a decisive answer to the whole question. The fact of the matter is that it is curious that not all those who argue in glowing speeches against Europe and against European notions can adhere to the views adopted by our Greco-Slavonic church. Invariably they plunge into some kind of Indo-Mongolian Asiaticism and are carried away by the teachings of Confucius, Buddha, or Tibetan Lamaism. Their alienation from Europe is directly proportional to their gravitation toward Asia. What does this mean? Let us admit that they are right in their view of Europe, that it is a great delusion for us. But why are they so fatally carried away by the other extreme — by this Asiaticism? And where have their Greco-Slavonic and Orthodox ideas disappeared to? No! Tell me! Where have they gone? And yet it is in these very ideas that one would expect to find the substance of the thing! There you are, you see. You may drive out nature by the door and it enters through the window. And nature, in this case, is the fact that no independent Greco-Slavonic type of historic culture exists at all; but there has been, is, and always will be Russia as the great borderland between Europe and Asia. Such being the actual position of our country, it is only too natural that we feel the influence of the Asiatic element to a much greater extent than does the rest of Europe, and this is all there is behind our imaginary originality. Byzantium herself was original not through anything of her own, but only because of an admixture of the Asiatic element. While with us — from time immemorial, and particularly since the days of the Mongolian yoke — this element has become a part of our nature, our second soul, so to speak, so that the Germans could say about us, sighing as they did so:

"Zwei Seelen wohnen, ach! in *ihrer* Brust
Die eine will sich von der andern trennen."
("Two souls, alas! dwell in *their* hearts
And the one desires to part from the other.")

It is impossible for us to get rid of this second — Asiatic — soul, nor is it desirable, for we owe a great deal to it. But in order to save ourselves from being torn to pieces in such a conflict as is suggested by the General, it has been necessary that one soul should establish a decisive supremacy over the other, and it stands to reason that this soul should be the better of the two — that it should develop an intellect which is really the more powerful, the more capable of further progress, and the more highly endowed with spiritual possibilities. Such supremacy was actually established at the time of Peter the Great. But, even after that, the ineradicable (though overpowered) affinity of our soul with Asia has led certain minds to meaningless dreams advocating some chimerical subversion of the great historical question which, in fact, has been finally settled once and forever. Hence Slavophilism, the theory of an original, autonomous type of historical culture and all the rest of it. As a matter of fact, we are *irrevocably European* but with an Asiatic sediment at the bottom of our soul. To me it is clear even grammatically. What is "Russian" in the grammatical sense? An adjective. But what is the noun to which it refers?

LADY – I think the noun is *person*: a Russian person, the Russian people.

POLITICIAN – No, that is too general and indefinite. Papuans and Eskimos are also people. I cannot agree in regarding as my noun what is common both to me and the Papuans and the Eskimos.

LADY – There are things, you know, which are common to all human beings: love, for instance.

POLITICIAN – Well, that is even more general. How can I regard love as my specific essence when I know that all other animals, and even miscreants, have it in their nature?

MR. Z. – The question is no doubt very complicated. I am, for example, a person of meek character and, as a lover, I am more like a white or blue-gray dove than I am like the Moor, Othello, though he also is called a person.

GENERAL – At a certain age, every sensible man is like the white doves. [12]

LADY – What are you talking about?

GENERAL – The pun in this case is not intended for you, but only for his Excellency and myself.

POLITICIAN – Let us drop this. We have joked enough. Surely we are not playing a French comedy on the stage of the Mikhailovksy Theater. I wished to say only that the correct noun for the adjective "Russian" is "European." We are *Russian Europeans*, as there are English, French, and German Europeans. If I feel myself to be a European, would it not be stupid of me to argue that I am some Slavo-Russ or Greco-Slav? I am as positively certain of being a European as I am of being a Russian. I can, and perhaps even must, pity and protect every human being and every animal too: "Blessed is he who shows mercy even to animals"; but I shall regard myself at one, *of the same family,* not with the Zulus or the Chinese, but only with the nations and people who have created and preserved all those treasures of culture which form my spiritual food and afford me my highest pleasures. Before all else, it was

---

[12] "White Doves" is the name of a Russian religious sect [accused of immoral tendencies] — Author.

necessary that these chosen nations should form and consolidate themselves and resist the onslaught of the lower elements. For this, war was necessary and war was a holy enterprise. But, at present, we possess the necessary form and strength and there is nothing we need fear except internal strife. So, now the time has arrived for peace and the peaceful expansion of European culture over all the world. All must become Europeans. The idea expressed by "European" must be as all-embracing as that expressed by "person" and the idea of the European civilized world identical with that of humanity. In this lies the meaning of history. At first there were only Greek Europeans. They were followed by Roman Europeans. Next there arose all kinds of others, first in the West, later in the East; then there came Russian Europeans; later, beyond the ocean, American Europeans; and now must come Europeans who are Turkish, Persian, Indian, Japanese, and possibly even Chinese. "European" is a notion with a definite content and an ever-expanding capacity. Note here one important distinction: every human being is just as much a human being as any other. Therefore, if we take as our noun this abstract symbol, we are bound to come to all-leveling equality, and the nation of Newton and Shakespeare will have to be valued no more highly than certain Papuans. This would be too absurd for words and subversive in practice. But, if my noun is not a human being in general, not that empty space with two feet, but a human being as a bearer of culture, that is, a European, then nothing is left to support this absurd universal equality. The idea of a *European*, or what is the same, the idea of *culture*, possesses a measure for defining the relative virtues or values of various races, nations, individuals. A sensible policy cannot but take into account all these variations in value. If it does not do so, if it, for instance, places on the same level a comparatively civilized Austria and some half-wild tribes of Herzegovina, this sort of thing will at once lead us to those stupid and dangerous adventures for which our last Mohicans of Slavophilism are still longing. *Il y a europeen et europeen*. Even after the cherished and, I hope, not far-distant hour has struck, when Europe or the civilized world will really coincide in extent with the total population of the world, even then there will remain in the unified and pacified realm of humanity all those natural and historically determined gradations and shades in the values of various cultures which will determine our relations with other nations. Even in the triumphant and all-embracing kingdom of the higher culture, just as much as in the kingdom of Heaven — one glory is of the sun, another glory of the moon, yet other glories of the stars, for one star differs from another in glory — this is, I believe, how it is said in the Catechism. And now, in these days when our goal, though near, is not quite realized, how much more is it necessary to guard ourselves from an all-leveling equality. At the present time, for instance, the papers have told us of more dissension between England and the Transvaal — that the Afrikaners are even threatening England with a war. [13] I can already see how all sorts of journalists and politicians in Russia, and most probably all over the Continent, will take up arms against England and will cry themselves hoarse in defense of those poor and oppressed Afrikaners. But it is the same as if our most esteemed, worthy, well-known and learned Mr. Martens, having entered a neighboring shop to buy something, was suddenly subjected to a violent attack by a dirty shopboy shouting: "The shop is mine; you are a stranger here; if you don't clear off I will strangle or kill you!" — by which time he is already strangling him. Of course, one would feel pity for our esteemed Mr. Martens for having fallen a victim to such a rascally trick. But if this actually happened, I should certainly feel some moral satisfaction if my esteemed friend, having properly

[13] The discussion took place in April 1898 — Author.

thrashed the rascal, had sent him by way of the police court to a home for young criminals. Instead of this, however, we see various respectable people encouraging the shopboy and spurring him on. "Clever boy! Fancy a little chap like that being plucky enough to tackle such a great hulking fellow! Go for him, Tommy; we will back you up when you want it!" How disgusting this is! Why, these Afrikaner keepers and breeders of cattle have not brains enough to proclaim themselves Dutchmen — which is what they are by blood. Holland is a real nation, highly cultured, with great merits to her credit. But no! They regard themselves as a separate nation; they want to create an African country of their own. The damned rascals!

LADY – In the first place, you need not swear. And in the second, tell me what this Transvaal is like, and what kind of people live in it.

MR. Z. – The people living there are a mongrel breed of Europeans and native Africans; they are neither white nor black; they are "buri" — Boers. [14]

LADY – A pun again, a *calembour*?

POLITICIAN – And not a very good one!

MR. Z. – What the brown *boers* are, such are also the calem *bours*. Though if you don't care for this color, they also have an *Orange* republic there.

POLITICIAN – Speaking seriously, these Boers are, of course, Europeans but poor specimens. Separated from their great metropolis, they have, to a great extent, lost their former culture. Surrounded by savages, they have become wilder and coarser themselves. Now, to place them on the same level as the English, and to go even so far as to wish them success in the struggle with England — *cela n'a pas de nom*!

LADY – Didn't your Europeans sympathize with the

---

[14] A play upon words. *Buri*, the Russian word for "Boer," also means "brown" — Translator.

Circassian mountain people when they fought Russia in defense of their independence? And are not Russians far more civilized than Circassians?

POLITICIAN – I would not care to enlarge upon the motives of this sympathy of Europe with the Circassian tribesmen. The only thing I will say is that we must assimilate the general European spirit and not be influenced by the accidental stupidities of this or that brand of European. From the bottom of my heart I regret, of course, that England, in order to pacify these conceited barbarians, will apparently be compelled to use such an obsolete and historically condemned weapon as war. But if war proves inevitable because of the degraded state of mind of these Zulus (I mean these Boers), encouraged as they are by that foolish envy of England nursed by the Continent, I shall, of course, eagerly wish the war to end as soon as possible with the complete defeat of these African ruffians so that nobody ever hears talk of their independence again. Should they prove successful — and owing to the distance of their country from England this is not altogether impossible — it would be a triumph of barbarism over culture; and, to me as a Russian, that is, as a European, the day that happened would be a day of deep national mourning.

MR. Z. (*to the General, in a low voice*) – Ah, how well statesmen speak. Altogether like that Frenchman: "*Ce sabre d'honneur est le plus beau jour de ma vie.*"

LADY – No, I can't agree with you. Why should we not sympathize with these transboers? We sympathize with William Tell, for instance, do we not?

POLITICIAN – Well, if only they had created their own poetical legend, had inspired such artists as Schiller and Rossini, and had produced from among themselves anybody equal to Jean Jacques Rousseau, or any other writers or scholars, then the thing would be quite different.

LADY – But all that kind of thing happens afterward. The Swiss themselves were shepherds like the Boers to begin with. Take other nations too. Were the Americans, when they rose against the English to win independence, in any way distinguished in culture? It is true they were not "Boers"; they were perhaps a little "red-skinned," and used to strip off each other's scalps, according to Captain Mayne Reid. And yet, even Lafayette sympathized with them, and he was right, because now, for instance, in Chicago, they have managed not only to unite all the religions, but they have exhibited them into the bargain. Nobody has ever seen such a thing before. Paris wanted to gather together all its religions for the coming exhibition but nothing came of it, as you doubtless know. One abbé, Victor Charbonel, strove particularly hard for this union of religions. He even wrote a few letters to me — he was so nice. But the religions refused to participate. Even the Great Rabbi declared: "For religion we have the Bible, and an exhibition has nothing to do with it." Poor Charbonel was in such despair that he renounced Christ and announced in the papers that he had retired from the service of religion and had acquired a profound respect for Renan. He ended very badly. According to somebody who wrote to me, he either got married or he took to drink. Then our Nepliuev also tried, and ended by becoming disappointed in every religion. He wrote to me once — he was such an idealist — to the effect that he relied only on a united humanity. But how can you show a united humanity at a Paris exhibition? It's a fantasy! However, the Americans managed their business very well indeed. Each creed sent them a clergyman. A Catholic bishop was made chairperson. He read them the Lord's Prayer in English, and the Buddhist and Chinese priests and idolators responded to him with complete courtesy: "Oh yes! Certainly, sir! We wish no one evil. We ask only one thing: keep your missionaries as far from our countries as you possibly can. Your religion is exceedingly good for you — and if you do not observe it, it is not our fault — but our religion is the best for us." The exhibition finished so well that there was not even a single fight! Everyone was astounded. Now you see how good the Americans have become! Perhaps the modern Afrikaners will in time be like these same Americans. Who knows?

POLITICIAN – Everything is possible. Even a street urchin may later become a scientist. But, before this happens, for his own benefit, you should give him more than one good hiding.

LADY – What language! *Décidément vous vous encanaillez.* This all comes from Monte Carlo! *Qui est-ce que vous fréquentez là bas? Les familles des croupiers sans doute.* Well, that concerns nobody but yourself. I would only ask you to prune your political wisdom a little bit, as you keep us from our dinner. It is time we finished.

POLITICIAN – I really wanted to sum up what I have said — to put head and tail together.

LADY – I have no faith in you. You will never finish of your own accord. Let me help you to explain your thought. You wanted to say, did you not, that times have changed; that formerly there was God (and war), but now, instead of God, there are culture and peace. Isn't that it?

POLITICIAN – I think it is near enough.

LADY – Good! Now, what God is I do not know, nor can I explain. But I feel it all the same. As to your culture, I have not the least feeling for it. Explain to me in a few words what it is.

POLITICIAN – What are the elements of culture? You know what culture is. It includes all the treasures of human thought and genius which have been created by the chosen spirits of the chosen nations.

LADY – But these "chosen spirits" and their creations differ alarmingly. You have, for instance, Voltaire and Bossuet, the Madonna and *Nana*, and Alfred de Musset and Bishop Philaret. How can you throw all these into one heap and set up this heap for yourself in place of God?

POLITICIAN – I was also going to say that we need not

worry ourselves about culture as an historical treasury. It has been created, it exists, and let us thank God for the fact. We may, perhaps, hope that there will be other Shakespeares and Newtons, but this problem is not within our power and presents no practical interest. There is, however, another side to culture, a practical one, or if you like a moral one, and this is what in private life we call politeness, civility. To the superficial eye it may appear unimportant, but it has an enormous and singular significance for the simple reason that it is the only quality that can be universal and obligatory. It is impossible to demand from anybody either the highest virtue or the highest intellect or genius. But it is possible and necessary to demand from everybody civility. It is that *minimum* of reasonableness and morality which allows people to live like true human beings. Politeness is not *the whole* of culture but it is a necessary *condition* of every form of cultured conduct, just as literacy, though not the sum total of education, is a necessary condition to it. Politeness is cultured conduct, *à l'usage de tout le monde*. And we are actually able to see how it spreads from private relationships among people of the same class to social relationships among different classes, and so to political or international relationships. Some of us can surely still remember how in our youth people of our class were allowed to treat the lower classes without any civility at all. Whereas, at present, a necessary and even compulsory politeness has overstepped this class boundary and is now on the way to overstepping international boundaries as well.

LADY – Please, speak briefly. I see what you are driving at. Peaceful politics among the States is the same as politeness among individuals. That is what you mean, isn't it?

POLITICIAN – You are quite correct. This is clear from the very words *politeness* and *politics*, which obviously are closely related to each other. A remarkable thing is that no special feelings are necessary for the expression of politeness, no such *goodwill*, as the General needlessly proposed. If I do not fall upon a person and do not furiously bite his head, this does not mean that I have any goodwill toward that person. On the contrary, I may nurse in my soul the most rancorous feelings but, as a cultured human being, I cannot but feel repulsion at the idea of biting anybody. And, what is more important, I understand full well that the result of it will be anything but savory and that, if I abstain from biting and instead treat this individual politely, I shall lose nothing and gain much. Similarly, whatever may be the antipathies existing between two nations, if they have reached a certain level of culture, they will never come to *voies de fait*, that is, to war, and for the patent reason that, in the first place, real war (not that portrayed in poetry and pictures, but as actually experienced) with all those corpses, foul-smelling wounds, crowds of rough and filthy men, the stoppage of the normal order of life, destruction of useful buildings and institutions, of bridges, railways, telegraphs — a thing as horrid as this is must be positively repulsive to a civilized nation, just as it is repulsive to us to see knocked-out eyes, broken jaws, and bitten-off noses. In the second place, at a certain stage of intellectual development, a nation understands how profitable it is to be civil to other nations and how damaging to its own interests it would be if it fought them. Here you have a number of gradations: the fist is more cultured than the teeth, the stick is more cultured than the fist, and the symbolic slap in the face is more cultured still. Wars, too, may be conducted in a more or less savage way. The European wars of the nineteenth century resemble more a formal duel between two respectable persons than a brawl between two drunken laborers. But even this is only a transitional stage. Note that even the duel is out of fashion in advanced countries, whereas backward Russia mourns her two greatest poets who have fallen in a duel. In more civilized France, the duel has long ago evolved into a bloodless relic of a bad and dead tradition. "*Quand on est mort c'est qu'on n'est plus en vie,*" M. de La Palisse would say. I am sure we shall still see duels together with war relegated forever to the archives of history. A compromise cannot last long here. Real culture requires that all *fighting* between people and nations be abolished. Peaceful politics are the measure and the outward sign of the progress of culture. This is why, however anxious I am to please the worthy General, I still stand by my statement that the literary agitation against war is a welcome and satisfying fact. This agitation not only precedes but actually expedites the final solution of a problem long since ripened. With all its peculiarities and exaggerations, this anti-war campaign acquires importance by its emphasizing in the public consciousness the main line of historical progress. A peaceful, "polite," universally profitable settlement of all international relations and conflicts — such is the fundamental principle of sound politics for civilized humanity. Ah! (*To Mr. Z.*) You want to say something?

MR. Z. – Oh, it's nothing. I only wanted to comment on your recent remark that peaceful politics is the symptom of progress. It reminds me that in Turgenev's *Smoke* some person, speaking just as reasonably, says, "Progress is a symptom." Don't you think, then, that peaceful politics becomes a symptom of a symptom?

POLITICIAN – Well, what of it? Of course, everything is relative. What is your point?

MR. Z. – My point is that if peaceful politics is merely a shadow of a shadow, is it worthwhile discussing it at such length? All this talk about shadowy progress? Would it not be much better to say frankly to humanity what Father Barsanophius said to the pious old lady: "You are old, you are feeble, and you will never be any better."

LADY – Well, it's too late to talk about this now. (*To the*

Politician) You see what a practical joke this politico-politeness of yours has played on you?

POLITICIAN – What?

LADY – Simply that your visit to Monte Carlo, or *par euphemisme*, to Nice, will have to be put off tomorrow!

POLITICIAN – Why?

LADY – Because these gentlemen here now want to reply to you. And as you have been speaking with such *prolixity* as to leave no time for their replies, they are entitled to do so tomorrow. And surely, at a time when a company of cultured people is busy refuting your arguments, you could scarcely permit yourself to indulge in more or less forbidden pleasures in the company of uneducated croupiers and their families? This would be the height of impoliteness. And what would be left then of your "obligatory minimum of morality"?

POLITICIAN – If that is the case, I must put off for one day my visit to Nice. I myself will be interested to hear what can be said against my axiom.

LADY – Splendid! Now I think everybody is really very hungry. But for our "culture" we would have long ago made a dash for the dining room.

POLITICIAN – *Il me semble du reste que la culture et l'art culinaire se marient très bien ensemble.*

LADY – Oh, no! I will not listen to stuff like this!

At this point, exchanging feeble witticisms, we hastily followed the lady of the house to the dinner awaiting us.

CHAPTER THREE
THE THIRD CONVERSATION
Audiatur et tertia *pars*

On the following day, by mutual consent, we met in the garden earlier than usual so that we might have more leisure to finish the discussion. Somehow all were in a more serious mood than the day before.

POLITICIAN (*to Mr. Z.*) – I believe you wanted to respond to the arguments I presented yesterday.

MR. Z. – Yes. I was interested in your definition of peaceful politics as a symptom of progress. It brought to my mind, as I said, the words of a character in Turgenev's *Smoke*, that "progress is a symptom." I don't know what that character meant exactly, but the literal meaning of these words is perfectly true. Progress is certainly a symptom.

POLITICIAN – A symptom of what?

MR. Z. – It is a pleasure to talk with clever people. [1] That is just the question to which I have been leading. I believe that progress — a visible and accelerated progress — is always a *symptom of the end*.

POLITICIAN – I can understand that, if we consider, for instance, progressive paralysis. Progress in that case is a symptom of the end. But why should the progress of culture and cultured life always be a symptom of the end?

[1] A Russian proverb — Translator.

116

Mr. Z. – Doubtless it is not so obvious as in the case of paralysis, but it is so all the same.

Politician – That you are convinced is clear enough, but what you are convinced of is not clear to me at all. Therefore, encouraged by your praise and to open our discussion, let me repeat the simple question which seemed to you so clever. You say, "a symptom of the end." The end of *what*, I ask you?

Mr. Z. – Naturally, the end of what we have been talking about. As you remember, we have been discussing the history of humanity, and that historical "process" which has doubtless been going on at an ever-increasing rate, and which I am certain is nearing its end.

Lady – *C'est la fin du monde, n'est-ce pas?* The argument is becoming a most curious one!

General – At last we have reached a most interesting subject.

Prince – You will not, of course, forget the Anti-Christ.

Mr. Z. – Certainly not. He takes the most prominent place in what I have to say.

Prince (*to Lady*) – Forgive me. I am just now terribly busy with very urgent matters. Though I am most anxious to hear the discussion on this extremely fascinating subject, I must, I am sorry to say, return home.

General – Return home? And what about whist?

Politician – I had a feeling from the very first day that some villainy or other was being prepared. Where religion is involved, never expect any good. *Tantum religio potuit suadere malorum.*

Prince – No villainy is to be perpetrated. I will try to come back at nine o'clock, but now I positively have no time.

Lady – Why this sudden urgency? How is it that you didn't inform us of such important matters before? No, I refuse to believe you. Candidly, it is the Anti-Christ that has scared you, isn't it?

PRINCE – Yesterday I heard so often that politeness is everything that, under the spell of this theory, I tried for the sake of civility to tell a lie. Now I see that I was wrong. I must tell you honestly that, though I am busy with many important matters, I am leaving this discussion mainly because I consider it impermissible to waste one's time discussing things which can be of interest only to Papuans and others like them.

POLITICIAN – Your grave sin of excessive civility is now expiated, it seems.

LADY – Why get angry? If we are stupid, enlighten us. Take me, for instance. I am not angry with you for having been called a Papuan. Why, even Papuans may have correct ideas. God makes infants wise. But if it is so difficult for you to hear about the Anti-Christ, we'll agree on this: Your villa is only a few steps from here. Go home to your work now, and return toward the end of the discussion — after the Anti-Christ . . .

PRINCE – Very well. I will return with pleasure.

(*The Prince left the company*)

GENERAL (*laughing*) – "The cat knows whose meat she has eaten."

LADY – What, you think our Prince is an Anti-Christ?

GENERAL – Well, not personally, not he personally; it will be a long time before he gets as far as that; but he is on the right track, all the same. As it is said in the Gospel of St. John: "You have heard, my little ones, that Anti-Christ is coming and there are many Anti-Christs now." So, one of these "many " . . .

LADY – One may find oneself among the "many" against one's wish. God will not punish the Prince for that. He has simply been led astray. He knows that he will never do anything remarkable, only walk around in a smart uniform as if he were transferred from the Army to the Guards. For a great General, all this makes no difference but it turns the head of a small officer.

POLITICIAN – The psychology is sound. Yet, I am unable to see why he should have become so angry when the Anti-Christ was mentioned. Take me, for instance. I have no faith whatever in things mystical and so it does not annoy me. On the contrary, it rather excites my curiosity from a general human standpoint. I know that, for many, it is something very serious. It is clear that some side of human nature has found its expression here, a side which is possibly atrophied in my consciousness but which, nevertheless, does not cease to preserve its objective interest even for me. I am a very bad judge of paintings, for instance I cannot draw even a straight line or a circle, nor am I able to perceive what is bad and what is good in the works of painters. Yet, I am interested in the art of painting from the standpoint of general education and general aesthetics.

LADY – It is difficult to be offended at such a harmless thing as art. But religion — you know you hate religion with all your heart. Only just now you quoted some Latin curse against it.

POLITICIAN – A curse! Good gracious! In the words of my favorite poet, Lucretius, I merely blamed religion for its bloodstained altars and cries of human sacrifices. I can hear an echo of this bloodthirstiness in the gloomy, intolerant utterances of the companion who has just left us. Still, religious ideas *per se* interest me very much — among others, the idea of the "Anti-Christ." Unfortunately, all I have been able to read on this subject is confined to the book by Renan, and he considers the question only in relation to the historical evidence which, in his opinion, points to Nero. But this is not sufficient. We know that the idea of the Anti-Christ was held by the Jews long before the time of Nero and was applied by them to King Antiochus Epiphanes. The Anti-Christ is still believed in by the

Russian "schismatics," so there must be some truth in the idea, after all.

GENERAL – The leisure your Excellency enjoys affords you every opportunity for the discussion of such high matters. But our poor Prince employs so much of his time in preaching evangelical morals that he is naturally prevented from pondering on Christ or Anti-Christ. Even for his whist he cannot get more than three hours a day. He is a person without pretense, and you must give him his due.

LADY – You are very severe on him, General. It is true that all his crowd seems unnatural. They are so miserable, too. You won't find any joy, satisfaction, or good humor in them. Yet is it not said in the Gospels that Christianity is the joy of the Holy Spirit?

GENERAL – Their situation is, indeed, very difficult: to be lacking in Christian spirit, and yet to pass themselves off as true Christians.

MR. Z. – Indeed. To pass themselves off as Christians *par excellence* without possessing what constitutes the real excellence of Christianity.

GENERAL – It seems to me that their sad situation is precisely that of the Anti-Christ whose situation, for the more clever and sensitive among us, is made the sadder by the awareness that, in the long run, providence cannot help them.

MR. Z. – In any case, it is beyond doubt that the Anti-Christianity which, according to the Bible, in both the Old and the New Testaments, marks the closing scene in the tragedy of history will be not a mere infidelity to or a denial of Christianity, nor simply the triumph of materialism or anything similar to it, but that it will be a religious *imposture*. The name of Christ will be arrogated by forces in humanity that in their practice and in their very essence are alien, even inimical, to Christ and his Spirit.

GENERAL – Naturally so. The Devil would not be what he is if he played an open game!

POLITICIAN – But I am afraid that all Christians may prove mere impostors and therefore, according to you, mere Anti-Christs. The only exception will be perhaps the unconscious masses of the people insofar as such still exist in the Christian world and a few originals like yourselves, ladies and gentlemen. Anyway, there can be no doubt that the name of "Anti-Christ" justly applies to those persons, here in France, as well as in our own country, who are particularly busy about Christianity, making of it their special occupation, and considering the name of Christian some sort of monopoly or privilege of their own. In our time such people fall in one of two categories equally alien, I hope, to the spirit of Christ. They are either mad slaughterers ready to revive at the drop of a hat the terrors of the inquisition and to organize religious massacres after the style of those "pious" abbés and "brave" "Catholic" officers who recently gave vent to their feelings on the occasion of celebrating some detected swindler;[2] or they are the new ascetics and celibates who have discovered virtue and conscience as they might discover some new America while, at the same time, losing their inner truthfulness and common sense. The former cause a moral repulsion; the latter make one yawn with boredom.

GENERAL – This is quite true. Even in the past, Christianity was unintelligible to some and hateful to others. But it remained to our time to make it either repulsive or so dull

___

[2] The Politician obviously refers here to the public subscription opened in commemoration of the "suicide" Henry. One French officer stated that he subscribed to the commemoration in the hope of seeing a new St. Bartholomew massacre; another officer wrote that he was looking forward to an early execution of all Protestants, Freemasons, and Jews. An abbé confessed that he lived in anticipation of that glorious time when the skin stripped off the Huguenots, the Masons, and the Jews will be used for making cheap carpets which, as a good Christian, he will always tread upon with his feet. These statements, among tens of thousands of others in a similar vein, were published in the paper, *La Libre Parole* — Author.

that it bores people to death. I can imagine how the Devil rubbed his hands and laughed until his stomach ached when he learned of his success. Good gracious me!

LADY – Well, is this Anti-Christ as you understand him?

MR. Z. – Some signs indicating his nature are given here, but he himself is still to come.

LADY – Then will you explain in the simplest way possible what the matter really is?

MR. Z. – I cannot, I am afraid, guarantee simplicity. One cannot simply have simplicity whenever one wishes just because one wishes it. And as for a false, artificial simplicity, nothing can be worse than that. There is an old saying which was often repeated by a friend of mine, now dead: *"Many a simplicity easily misleads."*

LADY – This is not so simple either.

GENERAL – I believe it is the same as the popular proverb: "Some simplicities are worse than thefts."

MR. Z. – You've guessed it!

LADY – Now I understand it, too.

MR. Z. – It is a pity, though, that one cannot explain everything about the Anti-Christ with proverbs.

LADY – Then explain as best you can.

MR. Z. – Very well, then. In the first place, tell me whether you recognize the existence and the power of evil in the world?

LADY – One would prefer not to recognize it, but one can hardly help doing so. Death alone would make one believe it: for death is an evil one cannot escape. I truly believe that "the last enemy to be destroyed will be death" but, until it is destroyed, it is clear that evil is not only strong in itself but even much stronger than good.

MR. Z. – General, what is your opinion?

GENERAL – I have never shut my eyes before bullets and shells and shall certainly not do so when faced with subtle questions. Certainly, evil is as real as good. There is God, but there is the Devil also — just so long, of course, as God tolerates him.

POLITICIAN – As for myself, for the moment I shall abstain from a definite answer. My view does not penetrate at all deeply into the matter, and the side of it which is clear to me I explained as best I could yesterday. But I am interested to know what other people think of it. I can understand perfectly well the Prince's mode of thought. In other words, I understand that there is no real thought in his case at all but only a naked pretension *qui n'a ni rime ni raison*. The positive religious view, however, is much more intelligent and more interesting. Yet, up to the present, my acquaintance with it has been confined to its official form — which affords me very little satisfaction indeed. I, therefore, should be very pleased to hear, instead of the vaporings of mealy-mouthed parsons, a natural human account.

MR. Z. – Of all the stars that rise on the mental horizon of one who carefully reads our sacred texts, I think there is none so clear, illuminating, and startling as that which shines forth in the words, "Thinkest thou that I come to bring peace on Earth? I come not to bring peace, but divisions." He came to bring *truth* to the earth, and truth, like good, before anything else *divides*.

LADY – This needs to be explained. If you are right, why is it that Christ is called the Prince of Peace, and why did he say that peacemakers will be called the children of God?

MR. Z. – You want me to reconcile these contradictory texts in a higher meaning?

LADY – I do wish it.

MR. Z. – Then, please note that the only way of reconciling these texts is by making a division between good or true peace and bad or false peace. This division was clearly pointed out by him who brought true peace and good enmity: "My peace I leave with you, My peace I give unto you. Not as the world giveth, give I unto you." Thus there is good peace — the peace of Christ, resting on the *division* that Christ came to bring to the world, namely, the division between good and evil, between truth and the lie — and there is bad peace, the peace of the world which tries to blend or to externally unite elements that are internally at war with one another.

LADY – But how can you show the difference between the good and the bad peace?

MR. Z. – In very much the same way as the General did when, the other day, he remarked jocularly that one may have a bad peace or a good peace like that, for instance, concluded by the treaties of Nystad and Kuchuk-Kainardji. Beneath this joke lies hidden a more general and profound meaning. As in the political struggle, so in the spiritual one; the good peace is that concluded when the object of the war is accomplished.

LADY – And what is the object of the war between good and evil? I am not even sure if it is even necessary for them to wage a war with each other, or whether such a thing as an actual conflict is possible between them — *corps à corps!* In an ordinary war, when one side becomes stronger, the opposing side looks for reinforcements, and the struggle has to be decided by pitched battles, with guns and bayonets. You will find nothing like this in the struggle between good and evil. In this struggle, when the good side becomes stronger, the bad side immediately weakens, and the struggle never leads to a real battle. So that all this talk of a war between good and evil must be taken only in a metaphorical sense. It is one's duty to foster the growth of good in man. Evil will then diminish as a matter of course.

MR. Z. – In other words, you believe that it is enough for kind people to grow still kinder so that wicked people will gradually lose their malice until finally they become as kind as the others?

LADY – I believe that is so.

MR. Z. – But do you know of any case when the kind-

ness of a kind person made the wicked person kind, or at
least less wicked?

LADY – No, candidly I do not. Neither have I seen or
heard of such cases . . . But, forgive me if I'm wrong, is not
what you have said just now similar to what you were
discussing with the Prince the other day? That even Christ,
however kind he was, could not convert the souls of Judas
and the bad thief? Do not forget that the Prince has still to
answer this.

MR. Z. – Well, since I don't believe the Prince to be the
Anti-Christ, I have little faith in his coming, and still less in
his theological presence of mind. However, in order to
relieve our discussion of the burden of this unsolved
question, I will state the objection which the Prince should
make *from his standpoint*. "Why did not Christ regenerate
the wicked souls of Judas and the others by the power of
his goodness?" For the simple reason, the answer would
run, that it was a dark time, and only a few choice souls
reached that degree of moral development which allows of
an adequate response to the inner power of truth. And
Judas and company were too "backward" for that. Further-
more, Jesus himself said to his disciples: "Deeds which I
do, you will do also, and even *more* than this you *will do*."
It follows that, at a higher stage of human moral progress,
such as we have reached at the present time, the true
disciples of Christ are able by the power of their kindness,
and by refusing to forcibly resist evil, to perform moral
miracles surpassing even those that were possible eighteen
centuries ago.

GENERAL – Just a moment! If they are *able* to perform
miracles, why don't they? Or have you seen some of these
new miracles? Even now, after "eighteen centuries of moral
progress in Christian consciousness," our Prince is still
unable to enlighten my dark soul. Just as I was a barbarian
before I met him, so I remain. I am just what I have always
been. After God and Russia, what I love most is military

work in general, and the artillery in particular. And in my lifetime I have met not only our Prince but other nonresisters as well, and some perhaps even stronger than he.

MR. Z. – Why assume such a personal attitude? And why hold me responsible? I only produced, on behalf of your absent opponent, a text from the Gospels which he had forgotten, and beyond that

Whether it is reason or unreason —
I do not answer for another's dream.

LADY – Now,I think I must defend our poor Prince. If he wanted to be really clever, he would say to the General: "I and those whom you have found to hold my views consider ourselves to be true disciples of Christ, but only in the sense of a general trend of thought and action, and not because we have any greater power of doing good. We are certain, however, that there are, or will shortly come, Christians more perfect than we, and they will be able to break through your wall of darkness."

MR. Z. – This answer would, no doubt, be very ingenious, as it would introduce an unknown quantity. But it can hardly be called serious. Suppose they say, or should say: "We can do nothing greater than what Christ did, nothing even equal to it, nothing even which falls little short of it"? What conclusion could be drawn from this according to the rules of sound logic?

GENERAL – Only one, it seems. Namely, that the words of Christ: "You will do what I did, and even more than this," were addressed not to these gentlemen, but to other persons who do not resemble them in the least.

LADY – Yet it is possible to imagine that some person will carry out Christ's commandment about loving his enemies and forgiving those who do wrong to him. And then he will, with the help of Christ himself, acquire the power through his own kindness to convert wicked souls into good ones.

Mr. Z. – Not so long ago an experiment was tried in this direction, and not only did it not realize its objective, but it actually proved the very opposite to what you are supposing now. There lived a man whose kindness knew no bounds. He not only forgave every wrong done to him, but for every evil returned deeds of kindness. Now, what do you suppose happened? Do you think he stirred the soul of his enemy and regenerated him morally? Alas! he only exasperated the evil spirit of the villain and died miserably by his hand.

Lady – What case are you talking about? What man was he? Where and when did he live?

Mr. Z. – Not so long ago, and in St. Petersburg. I thought you knew him. He was the court chamberlain, M. Delarue.

Lady – I have never heard of him, though I think I can count on my fingers all the leading people of the city.

Politician – Neither can I recollect him. But what is the story about this chamberlain?

Mr. Z. – It has been splendidly told in an unpublished poem by Count Alexis Tolstoy.

Lady – Unpublished? Then it is sure to be a farce. What can it have to do with the serious problems we are discussing?

Mr. Z. – I can assure you, Madame, that, farcical though it is in its form, it contains a very serious story, and, what is more to the point, one true to life. At any rate, the actual relationship between kindness and wickedness in human life is portrayed in these amusing verses with much greater skill than I could ever show in my serious prose. Moreover, when the heroes of some world famous popular novels, in which the black soil of psychology is skillfully and seriously ploughed, have become mere literary reminiscences for bibliophiles, I am certain that this farce which, in an exaggerated and wildly caricatured form, plumbs the very depth of the moral problem, will retain all its artistic and philosophic truth.

LADY – I don't believe in your paradoxes. You are seized with the spirit of contradiction, and willfully defy public opinion.

MR. Z. – I should probably "defy" it if it really existed. Still, I am going to tell you the story of court chamberlain Delarue, since you do not know it, and I happen to remember it by heart:

> The wicked robber drove his dagger
> Deep into the breast of Delarue,
> Who, for his part, lifted his hat and said,
> "Dear Sir, thank you!"
> In the left side then the robber struck again
> His dreadful dagger,
> And Delarue said, "What a splendid weapon,
> Remarkably good!"
> The villain now struck the Chamberlain's right side,
> Wounding him in the chest;
> But Delarue with a gentle smile said,
> "Naughty fellow, what a jest!"
> The villain next raised his dagger up
> Striking in a hundred places;
> Said Delarue: "How time's flying!
> Will you stay to tea?"
>
> The wicked man sobbed and fell upon his knees,
> Trembling like a leaf.
> Said Delarue,"For God's sake, man, get off the floor!"
> Said Delarue,"It's dirty."
>
> But now the villain lay before him grieving and
>   repentant,

Contritely he confessed his wrong.
Then Delarue lifted up the prostrate man
With arms both strong and loving.
"I see you weep. For what? No use in crying over
Such a trifle. My dear sir!
I'll speak to the Tsar on your behalf. A pension
He will give you.
The order of Stanislas I'll pin upon your breast —
Does that make you proud? —
I can secure these things, I have the Tsar's ear,
His chief chamberlain am I.
Or would you care to wed my daughter, Dunya?
If that is your desire
I'll settle ten thousand pounds in notes on you,
A dowry from her father.

And now, I pray you, accept my portrait here,
If you'll be so kind:
A token, it shows my love for you.
It isn't framed — But I know you won't mind."

The villain's face grew evil now, bitterer than pepper:
"Is this then my fate,
To owe my life and all I have to a man
Who repays my hate with love?"

The lofty spirit thus the base age discovers,
Revealing its disgrace.
Assassins may forgive the gift of a portrait;
But not of a pension and a place.
The fires of envy smolder in this vile heart's depths,
Dark altars of shame;
And while as yet the ribbon's new on his shoulder,
It bursts into flame.

So filled with devilish malice he dips his dagger

In poison;
He lies in wait for Delarue and deals him
A blow deep and sure.
Down falls Delarue to the ground, in his armchair
He can no longer remain.
Upstairs flies the villain, and there poor Dunya falls
Despoiled as his prize.

The villain fled to Tambov where as Governor
He is now justly esteemed;
And later, in Moscow, as Senator, he is deemed by all
Worthy of the highest honors;
There he soon attained to honorable membership
In the Councils of the State;
Oh! what an example he is to all of us!
Oh! what a fate!

LADY – Oh, how charming, how sweet! I never expected anything so delightful!

POLITICIAN – Very fine indeed. Some expressions are really masterful.

MR. Z. – But note how true to life all this is. Delarue is not a specimen of that "purified virtue" which one never meets in nature. He is a real man with all the human weaknesses. He is vain ("I am a chamberlain," he says) and fond of money (he has managed to save ten thousand pounds); while his fantastic immunity to the stabs of the villain's dagger is, of course, merely an obvious symbol of his infinitely good humor, invincible, even insensitive to all wrongs — a trait also to be met with in life, though comparatively seldom. Delarue is not a personification of virtue but a naturally kindhearted man whose kindness overpowered all his bad qualities, driving them to the surface of his soul and revealing them there in the form of inoffensive weaknesses. The "villain" also is not the conventional essence of vice but the normal mixture of good and evil qualities. The evil of envy, however, rooted itself in the very depth of his soul and forced out all the good in him to the very *epidermis* of his soul, so to speak, where the kindness became a sort of very active but superficial sensitivity. When Delarue replies to a number of offensive actions with polite words and with an invitation to tea, the villain's sensitivity is greatly moved by these acts of gentleness, and he descends to a climax of repentance. But when, later, the chamberlain's civility is changed into the sincere sympathy of a deeply good-natured man who retaliates the evil done, not with the seeming kindness of nice words and gestures, but with the actual good of practical help — when, I say, Delarue shows interest in the actual situation of his enemy, is willing to share his fortune with him, to secure an official post for him, and even to provide him with family happiness — then this *real* kindness, penetrating into the deeper moral strata of the villain, reveals his inner moral emptiness and, when it reaches the very bottom of his soul, it arouses the slumbering crocodile of envy. It is not the kindness of Delarue that excites the envy of the villain — as you have seen, he can also be kind, and when he cried, pitifully wringing his hands, doubtless he was conscious of this. What did excite his envy was the — for him — unattainable infinite vastness and *simple seriousness* of that kindness:

> Assassins may forgive the gift of a portrait;
> But not of a pension and a place.

Is it not realistic? Do we not see this in everyday life? The same moisture of vivifying rain causes the development of healing powers in some herbs and of poison in others. In the same way, a real act of kindness, after all, only helps to develop good in the good human being and evil in the evil one. If so, how can we — have we even the right to — let loose our kind sentiments without choice and distinction?

Can we praise parents who zealously water with their good watering can the poisonous flowers growing in their garden where their children play? I ask you, why was Dunya ruined?

General – I agree! Had Delarue given a good drubbing to the villain and chucked him out afterward, the fellow would not have had time for fooling upstairs.

Mr. Z. – I am prepared to admit that he had the right to sacrifice *himself* to his kindness. Just as in the past there were martyrs of faith, so in our time I can admit there must be martyrs of kindness. But what, I ask you, should be done with Dunya? You know, she is silly and young and cannot prove anything, nor does she wish to prove any thing, by her own example. Is it possible, then, not to pity her?

Politician – I suppose it is not. But I am even more sorry for the fact that the Anti-Christ seems to have fled to Tambov with the villain.

Mr. Z. – Never mind, your Excellency. We'll catch him soon enough! Yesterday you were pleased to point out the meaning of history by reference to the fact that natural humanity (at first consisting of a great number of more or less savage races, alien to each other, partly ignorant of each other, partly actually engaged in mutual hostilities) gradually evolved from within itself its best and most educated part — the civilized or European world, which ever grows and spreads until it embraces all other groups that lag behind in this historical development, blending them into one peaceful and harmonious international whole. The establishment of a permanent international peace — this is your formula, is it not?

Politician – It is. And this formula, in its approaching and not too far distant realization, will stand for a much greater achievement in the real progress of culture than it may seem to stand for at present. Merely reflect on what quantity of evil will die an inevitable death, and what quantity of good will appear and grow. This is the very nature of things. What great powers will be released for productive work, what progress will be seen in science and art, industry and trade!

MR. Z. – And do you include in the coming achievements of culture a total extinction of diseases and death?

POLITICIAN – Of course . . . to some extent. Quite a good deal has already been done in the way of sanitation, hygienics, antiseptics . . . organo-therapeutics . . .

MR. Z. – Don't you think that these undeniable successes in the positive direction are fully counterbalanced by equally undeniable increases in neuropathic and psychopathic symptoms of the degeneration accompanying the advance of culture?

POLITICIAN – What criteria have we for estimating these?

MR. Z. – At any rate, it is absolutely certain that though the *plus* may grow, the *minus* grows as well, and the result obtained is something very near to *nil*. This is so at least far as diseases are concerned. As to death, it seems nothing but *nil* has ever been obtained in the progress of culture.

POLITICIAN – But the progress of culture never sets before itself such an objective as the extinction of death.

MR. Z. – I know it does not. And for this reason it cannot be rated very high. Just suppose I know for certain that I myself and all that is dear to me are to disappear forever. Would it not, in such a case, be quite immaterial to me whether somewhere in the world certain races are fighting with each other or whether they are living in peace; whether they are civilized or savage, polite or impolite?

POLITICIAN – Well, it would be immaterial, no doubt, from the standpoint of pure egotism.

MR. Z. – Why only of egotism? It would be immaterial from any point of view. Death equalizes everything. In the face of death, egotism and altruism are equally senseless.

POLITICIAN – So be it. But the senselessness of egotism does not prevent us from being egotists. Similarly, altruism, insofar as it is possible at all, can do quite well without any good reasons, and your argument about death does not touch it in any way. I am aware that my children and grandchildren are destined to die, but this does not interfere with my efforts to ensure their well-being just as much as if it were to be permanent. I exert myself for their benefit because, in the first place, I love them, and it gives me a moral satisfaction to devote my life to them. "I find taste in it." It is as clear as daylight.

LADY – Everything is all right so long as everything goes right though, even then, the thought of death sometimes comes to one's mind. But what satisfaction, what taste can one enjoy when all sorts of mishaps begin to happen to one's children? It is just like water lilies on a swamp: you grab hold of one and you go to the bottom yourself.

MR. Z. – Apart from this, you can and must think of your children and grandchildren *quand même*, without solving or even attempting to solve the question whether your efforts can do them any real and final good. You take trouble about them, not for the sake of any definite objective, but *because* you love them so dearly. Human beings who do not yet exist cannot excite such love, and here the question put by our intellect as to the *final* meaning or aim of our cares acquires its full importance. If the answer to this question is death, if the final result of your progress and your culture is the death of one and all, it is then clear that every kind of activity for the sake of progress and civilization is without purpose or meaning.

(*Here Mr. Z. interrupted his speech, and we all turned our heads toward the gate which clicked. For a few seconds we remained in astonished silence as we watched the Prince, who had entered the garden, walking unsteadily and with uneven steps toward us.*)

LADY – Oh! And we have not even started the discussion about the Anti-Christ.

PRINCE – It makes no difference. I changed my mind. I think I should not have shown any ill-feeling toward the errors of my neighbors before I had heard their argument.

LADY (*in a triumphant voice to the General*) – You see! What do you say now?

GENERAL (*sharply*) – Nothing!

MR. Z. – You arrived just in time. We are discussing the question whether it is worthwhile to trouble about progress if we know that the end of it is always death for everyone, whether a native or the highly educated European of the future. What do your theories say about this?

PRINCE – True Christian doctrine does not even admit of stating the question in this way. The Gospel approach is most strikingly and forcefully expressed in the parable of the husbandmen. The husbandmen came to imagine that the garden, into which they had been sent to work for their lord, was their own property; that everything in the garden was made for them; and that the only thing they had to do was to enjoy their life there, forgetting their lord and killing everybody who dared to remind them of his existence and of their duties toward him. Like those husbandmen, nearly all people in our time live in the absurd belief that they themselves are the lords of their life and that it has been given them for their enjoyment. The absurdity of this is obvious. For, if we have been sent here, it was at someone's behest and for some purpose. But we have decided that we are like mushrooms: that we were born and live only for our own pleasure; and it is clear that this is as bad for us as it would be bad for the worker who does not carry out his master's will. In our case, the master's will is expressed in the teaching of Christ. Let people only carry out this teaching and the Kingdom of God will be established on earth and human beings will obtain the greatest good that they are capable of securing. Everything lies in this. *Seek for the Kingdom of God, and His truth and the rest will come to you of itself.* We seek for *the rest* and do not find it; and not only do we not establish the Kingdom of God but we actually destroy it by our various States, armies, courts, universities, and factories.

GENERAL – Now the machine has been wound up.

POLITICIAN (*to the Prince*) – Have you finished?

PRINCE – Yes, I have.

POLITICIAN – I must tell you that your solution of the question seems to me absolutely incomprehensible. You speak as though about something, trying to prove and to explain something, wanting to convince us of something, and yet everything you say is a series of arbitrary and mutually disconnected statements. You say, for instance: "If we have been sent here, this was done at someone's behest and for some purpose." This seems to be your main idea. But where did you learn that we have been sent here for a definite purpose? Who told you this? That we exist here on earth — this is an indisputable fact; but that our existence is some sort of ambassadorship — for asserting this you have no ground whatsoever. When, for example, I was an ambassador in my younger days, I knew it for certain, as I also knew by whom and for what I was sent — first, because I had incontestable documents stating it; second, because I had had a personal audience with the late Emperor, Alexander II, and had received instructions in person from his Imperial Majesty; and, third, because every quarter I was paid ten thousand rubles in sterling gold. Now, if, instead of all that, some stranger had come up to me in the street and said that I had been appointed an ambassador to be sent to some place, for some purpose or other — well, I should at once have looked round to see if I could find a policeman who would protect me from a maniac capable, perhaps, even of committing an assault on my person. As regards the present case, you will admit that you have no incontestable documents from your supposed lord, that you have had no personal audience with him, and that no salary is being paid to you. And you call yourself an ambassador! And this goes not only for yourself but for everybody in existence — you have declared everybody to be either an ambassador or a husbandman. Have you any right to make such statements? Or any ground? No, I refuse to understand it. It seems to me a kind of rhetorical improvisation *très mal inspirée d'ailleurs*.

LADY – Now you are pretending again! How bad of you! You understand only too well that the Prince did not think of refuting your atheism but meant to state the commonly accepted Christian opinion that we all depend on God and are obliged to serve him.

POLITICIAN – I cannot understand a service without a salary. And if it proves that the salary here is one and the same for everybody — death — well then, I present my compliments . . .

LADY – But you will die in any case, and nobody will ask for your consent.

POLITICIAN – It is precisely this very "in any case" that proves that life is not service. If no consent of mine is required for my death anymore than for my birth, then I prefer to see in death and life what is actually there in them, a natural necessity, and not some imaginary service to some unknown master. So my conclusion is this: Live while you live, and endeavor to live in the best and most intelligent manner; and the condition of good and intelligent life is peaceful culture. However, I am of the opinion that, even on the basis of the Christian doctrine, the sham solution of the problem suggested by the Prince will not stand the slightest criticism. But let others, more competent than myself, speak of this.

GENERAL – Of course, it is no solution. It is merely a verbal way of getting round the question. Just as if I took out a map and, having surrounded an enemy's pencilled fortress with my pencilled battalions, then imagined that I had actually taken the actual fortress. Things of this kind

have really happened, you know, as the popular soldiers'
song tells: —

> Of this month scarce three days had passed
> When devil-driven forth we went
> to occupy the hilltops.

> Princes and counts came to see us then,
> And surveyors who made great maps
> On sheets of fine white paper.

> On paper, hills are smooth no doubt,
> For all the ravines are simply left out!
> But it was these we had to walk on!

The result of which is also well known: —

> At last we to the summit got
> And counted up our little lot;
> Of all our regiments there remained
> No more than a couple of battalions!

PRINCE – This is beyond me! Is this all you can answer to
what I have been saying here?

GENERAL – One thing in what you have been saying here
seemed to me particularly obscure — your remarks about
mushrooms, that these live for their own enjoyment. My
impression has always been that they live for the enjoyment of those who like to eat mushrooms — with cream or
in mushroom pies. Now, if your Kingdom of God on earth
leaves death just as it is, it follows that people, quite
independently of their will, live now and will continue to
live in your Kingdom of God just like mushrooms — and
not those jolly imaginary mushrooms, but the actual ones
cooked in a pan. The end of people in this earthly Kingdom
of God is also to be eaten up by death.

LADY – The Prince didn't say so.

GENERAL – Not that or anything else. But what is the reason for such reticence concerning the most important point?

MR. Z. – Before we raise this question, I would like to learn the source of this parable in which you, Prince, expressed your view. Or is it entirely your own composition?

PRINCE – My own composition? Why, it is taken from the Gospels!

MR. Z. – Oh no, no, you are surely wrong! You won't find this parable in any of the Gospels.

LADY – Good gracious! Why are you trying to confuse the Prince? You know that there is a parable about husbandmen in the Gospels; surely you do.

MR. Z. – Superficially — in the outer story — there is something like it, but it is entirely different both in narrative and in the meaning which is immediately thereafter pointed out.

LADY – Surely not! I think it is exactly the same parable. You are trying to be too clever. I don't trust a single word of yours.

MR. Z. – There is no need to take my word for it: the book is in my pocket. (*Here Mr. Z. got out a small pocket edition of the Gospels and began turning over the pages.*) The parable of the husbandmen can be found told by three evangelists: Saints Matthew, Mark, and Luke, but all of them state it in very much the same form. It will, therefore, be sufficient to quote it from the more elaborate Gospel of St. Luke. It is in Chapter XX, in which Christ's last sermon to the people is given. The drama is nearing its end, and it is now narrated (end of Chapter XIX and beginning of Chapter XX) how the enemies of Christ — the party of chief priests and scribes — made an open and decisive attack upon him, demanding publicly that he should state his authority and explain by what right and by virtue of what power he was acting. But I think I had better read it to you. (*Reads.*) "And he taught daily in the Temple. But the chief priests and the scribes and the chief of the people sought to destroy him. And could not find what they might do; for all the people were very attentive to hear him. And it came to pass, that on one of those days, as he taught the people in the Temple, and preached the Gospel, the chief priests and the scribes came upon him with the elders. And spake unto him, saying: Tell us, by what authority doest thou these things? Or who is he that gave thee this authority? And he answered and said unto them, I will also ask you one thing, and answer me: The baptism of John, was it from Heaven or of men? And they reasoned with themselves, saying, If we shall say, From Heaven, he will say, Why then believed ye him not? But and if we say, Of men, all the people will stone us; for they be persuaded that John was a prophet. And they answered, that they could not tell whence it was: And Jesus said unto them, Neither tell I you by what authority I do these things . . ."

Lady – And why do you read all this? It was quite right of Christ not to answer when he was questioned by these men. But what has it to do with the husbandmen?

Mr. Z. – A little patience. It all leads to the same thing. Besides, you are wrong when you say that Christ did not answer. He answered most definitely — and even doubly: he quoted such a witness of his authority as the questioners dared not reject, and next proved that they themselves had no proper authority or right over him, as they acted only out of fear of the people, afraid for their lives, adapting themselves to the opinions of the mob. Real authority is that which does not follow others, but itself leads them forward. Fearing and obeying the people, these men revealed that the real authority had deserted them and now belonged to the people. It is to these latter that Christ now addresses himself in order to accuse them of resisting him. In this accusation of the unworthy leaders of the Jewish nation for their resistance to the Messiah — in this lies the whole purport of the Gospel parable of the husbandmen, as you will presently see for yourself. (*Reads*): "Then began He to speak to the *people* this parable:

A certain man planted a vineyard, and let it forth to husbandmen, and went into a far country for a long time. And at the season he sent a servant to the husbandmen, that they should give him of the fruit of the vineyard: but the husbandmen beat him, and sent him away empty. And again he sent another servant, and they beat him also, and entreated him shamefully, and sent him away empty. And again he sent a third: and they wounded him also, and cast him out. Then said the lord of the vineyard, What shall I do? I will send my beloved son: it may be they will reverence him when they see him. But when the husbandmen saw him, they reasoned among themselves, saying, This is the heir: come, let us kill him, that the inheritance may be ours. So they cast him out of the vineyard, and killed him. What, therefore, shall the lord of the vineyard do unto them? He shall come and destroy these husbandmen and shall give the vineyard to others.

And when they heard it, they said, God forbid. And He beheld them and said, What is this then that is written, The stone which the builders rejected, the same is become the head of the corner? Whosoever shall fall upon that stone shall be broken; but on whomsoever it shall fall, it will grind him to powder. And the chief priests and the scribes that same hour sought to lay hands on Him; for they feared the people: for they perceived that He had spoken this parable against them." About whom, then, and about what, I ask you, was the parable of the vineyard told?

PRINCE – I can't understand what it is you are driving at. The Judaean chief priests and scribes felt offended because they were, and knew themselves to be, the representatives of those wicked laypeople of which the parable spoke.

MR. Z. – But of what was it they were accused in the parable?

PRINCE – Of not carrying out the true teaching.

POLITICIAN – I think the whole thing is clear enough. The scoundrels lived like mushrooms for their own enjoyment, smoked tobacco, drank spirits, ate slaughtered meat, and even treated their god to it. Besides which, they got married, took the chair in the courts, and engaged in warfare.

LADY – Do you really think that it suits your age and position to indulge in such sneering outbursts? Don't listen to him, Prince. We both want to speak seriously. Now tell me this. After all, according to the parable, the husbandmen were destroyed because they had killed the lord's son and heir — and this is the main point in the Gospel. Why, then, do you omit it?

PRINCE – I leave it out for the simple reason that it refers to the personal fate of Christ, which, naturally, has its own importance and interest but is, after all, unessential to that which is one and the same for everybody.

LADY – Which is . . .?

PRINCE – The carrying out of the Gospel teaching, by means of which the Kingdom of God and his justice are attained.

LADY – Just one second. I feel everything is now mixed up in my head . . . What is it we are talking about? Ah! (*To Mr. Z.*) You have the Gospel in your hand, so you will perhaps tell us what follows the parable in that particular chapter.

MR. Z. (*Turning over the pages*) – It is also stated there that it is necessary that those things which be Caesar's should be rendered to Caesar, and that the dead will be raised because God is a God not of the dead but of the living. Then there is given a proof that Christ is not David's son but the Son of God. Finally, the last two verses are against the hypocrisy and vanity of the Scribes.

LADY – You see, Prince, these are also Gospel teachings: that the State should be recognized in lay matters, that we should believe in the resurrection of the dead, and that Christ is not an ordinary man but God's Son.

PRINCE – It is impossible to conclude anything from a single chapter composed no one knows when or by whom.

LADY – Oh, no! I know even without looking up the matter in books that, not just in this single chapter, but in all four Gospels, a great deal is said about both resurrection and Christ's divinity — particularly in St. John's Gospel, which is even read at funeral services.

MR. Z. – As to the uncertainty of the origin of the Gospels, it is now recognized, even by the liberal German critics, that all the four Gospels were composed in the time of the Apostles, that is, in the first century.

POLITICIAN – Why, even the thirteenth edition of *"La Vie de Jésus"* I have noticed contains a retraction of what had originally been said about the fourth gospel.

MR. Z. – One must not lag behind one's teachers. But the principal difficulty, Prince, is that whatever our four Gospels may be, whenever and by whomsoever they were composed, there is no other gospel extant more trustworthy and more in agreement with your "teaching" than this.

GENERAL – Who told you it does not exist? Why, there is the fifth one, which contains nothing of Christ but the *teaching* — about slaughtered meat and military service.

LADY – You too? You should be ashamed of yourself. Remember that the more you and your political ally tease the Prince, the more support I shall give him. I am sure, Prince, that you want to look upon Christianity from its best side, and that your gospel, though not the same as ours, is similar to the books composed in times gone by: something like "L'Esprit de M. de Montesquieu," "L'Esprit de Fénelon," etc. In the same way, you or your teachers wanted to compose "L'Esprit de l'Evangile." It is only a great pity that nobody of your persuasion has done it in a small book which could be called *"The Spirit of Christianity according to the teaching of so-and-so."* You should have some sort of a catechism so that we simple folk should not lose the thread in all these intricacies. One moment we are told that the whole thing is in the Sermon on the Mount; another moment we are told that we must first of all labor in the sweat of our brow in agricultural work. The Gospel does not say this anywhere, but Genesis does, where it speaks of giving birth in pains — but this is not a commandment, only a sad fate. At one moment we are told that we must give everything we have to the poor. The next moment, that we must not give anything to anybody since money is evil, and it is bad to do evil to others, save to ourselves and our family. For others we must labor. Then again we are told to do nothing but contemplate. And yet again, that the mission of women is to give birth to as many healthy children as possible. And then, suddenly, that nothing of the kind is necessary. Then that we must not eat meat — this is the first stage, and why the first nobody can tell. We must give up now spirits and smoking, now pancakes. Last comes the objection to military service — that all evil is due to it, and that the first duty of a Christian is to refuse it; and whoever has not been officially recruited is, of course, holy as he is. Perhaps I am talking nonsense, but this is not my fault. It is absolutely impossible for me to make head or tail of it all.

PRINCE – I also think that we require a sensible summary of the true teaching. I believe it is being prepared now.

LADY – Before it is prepared, tell me briefly what is, in your opinion, the essence of the Gospel.

PRINCE – Surely, it is clear enough. It is the great principle of not resisting evil by force.

POLITICIAN – And how do you deduce from this the smoking?

PRINCE – What smoking?

POLITICIAN – Dear me! I ask what connection is there

between the principle of nonresistance to evil and the rules of abstinence from tobacco, wine, meat, and amorous indulgence?

PRINCE – It seems the connection is obvious: all these vicious habits stupefy a person — stifling the demands of one's intelligence and conscience. This is why soldiers generally go to war in a state of drunkenness.

MR. Z. – Particularly to an unsuccessful war. But we may leave this aside. The rule of not resisting evil has its own importance apart from the question of whether it justifies ascetic life or does not. According to you, if we do not resist evil by force, evil will immediately disappear. It follows that evil exists only by our resistance or by those measures which we take against it, but has no real power of its own. Properly speaking, there is no evil at all. It appears only because of our erroneous belief that it does exist and because we begin to act in accordance with that presumption. Isn't that so?

PRINCE – No doubt it is.

MR. Z. – But, if evil does not exist in reality, how will you explain the startling failure of Christ's cause in history? From your point of view, it has, of course, proved an utter failure, so that no good results can be credited to it, while the harm done has undoubtedly far exceeded its good effects.

PRINCE – How is that?

MR. Z. – A strange question to ask, to be sure! Well, if you do not understand it, we will examine it in a methodical way. You agree that Christ preached true good in a more clear, powerful, and consistent way than anybody else?

PRINCE – He did.

MR. Z. – And the true good consists in not opposing evil with force — so-called evil, imaginary evil that is, since there is no actual evil.

PRINCE – Yes.

MR. Z. – Christ not only preached but carried out to the final end the demands of this good by suffering without any resistance the torments of crucifixion. Christ, according to you, died and did not rise. Very well. Thousands of his followers suffered the same. Very well again. But now, what has been the result of it all?

PRINCE – Would you like to see all these martyrs, as a reward for their deeds, crowned by angels with brilliant wreaths and reclining somewhere under the trees in Elysian gardens?

MR. Z. – No, there is no need for that. Of course we all, including yourself, I hope, wish all that is best and most pleasant to our neighbors, both living and dead. But the question is not of our wishes but of what has actually resulted from the preaching and sacrifice of Christ and his followers.

PRINCE – Resulted for whom? For themselves?

MR. Z. – What resulted for themselves everybody knows: a painful death. But moral heroes as they were, they willingly accepted it, not in order to get brilliant wreaths for themselves but to secure true benefit for others, for the whole of humanity. Now I ask you, what are the benefits earned for humanity through their martyrdom? In the words of an old saying, "The blood of martyrs is the seed of the Church." In point of fact, it is quite true. But your contention is that the Church has been nothing but the distortion and ruin of true Christianity which was, as a result, entirely forgotten by humanity, so that it became necessary after eighteen centuries to restore everything from the very beginning without any guarantee of greater success; in other words, quite hopelessly.

PRINCE – Why hopelessly?

MR. Z. – Because you yourself have admitted that Christ and the first Christians gave their whole souls and sacrificed their lives for their cause and, if, this notwithstanding, nothing resulted from their efforts, what grounds have you then for hoping for any other result? There is only one indubitable and permanent end to all such practice of good, the same for those who initiated it and for those who distorted and ruined it and for those who have been restoring it. They all, according to you, died in the past, die in the present, will die in the future. And from the practice of good, the preaching of truth, nothing but death ever came, comes, or promises to come. Well, what is the meaning of it all? Isn't it strange that nonexistent evil always triumphs and good always falls through to nothingness?

LADY – Do not evil people die as well?

MR. Z. – Very much so. But the point is that the power of evil is only *confirmed* by the reign of death, whereas the power of good is, on the contrary, disproved. Indeed, evil is *obviously* more powerful than good, and if the *obvious* is the only thing real, then you cannot but admit that the world is the work of the evil power. How some people, while recognizing only obvious reality, and therefore admitting the predominance of evil over good, maintain at the same time that evil does not exist and that, consequently, there is no need for fighting it — this passes my understanding, and I expect the Prince to help me in this difficulty.

POLITICIAN – You had better give us first your own method of getting out of it.

MR. Z. – It is quite simple. Evil really exists, and it finds its expression not only in the deficiency of good but in the positive resistance and predominance of the lower qualities over the higher ones in all spheres of being. There is an individual evil in the great majority of people. This occurs when the lower side of human beings, their animal and bestial passions, resist the better impulses of the soul, *overpowering them.* And there is a social evil, when the human crowd, individually enslaved by evil, resists the salutary efforts of the few better men and eventually overpowers them. There is, lastly, a physical evil in humanity, when the baser material constituents of the human body resist the living and enlightening power that binds them together into a beautiful form of organism and resist and break the form, destroying the real basis of the higher life. This is the *extreme* evil, called death. And were we compelled to recognize the victory of this extreme physical evil as final and absolute, then no imaginary victories of good in the individual and social spheres could be considered real successes. Let us, indeed, imagine that a good man, say Socrates, not only triumphed over his inner forces — the bad passions — but also succeeded in convincing and reforming his social foes, in reconstructing the Hellenic "politeia." Now, what would be the use of this ephemeral and superficial victory over evil if evil is allowed finally to triumph over the very foundations of life in the deepest strata of being, bringing for both the reformer and the reformed but one end: death? By what logic would it be possible to appraise highly the moral victories of Socrates' good over the moral microbes of bad passions within him and over the social microbes of the Athenian *agora*, if the real victors would be, after all, the much worse, baser, and coarser microbes of physical decomposition? Here, no moral verbiage will protect you against utter pessimism and despair.

POLITICIAN – We have heard this before. What is your remedy against despair?

MR. Z. – Our remedy is one: actual resurrection. We know that the struggle between good and evil is not confined only to soul or society but is carried on in the deeper spheres of the physical world. We have one victory of the good power of life already recorded in the past — one personal resurrection. We can thus look forward to future victories involving the collective resurrection of all. Here even evil is given its reason or the final explanation of its existence in that it serves to enhance the triumph, realization, and power of good: if death is more powerful than mortal life, resurrection to eternal life is even more powerful than both of them. The Kingdom of God is the kingdom of life triumphing through resurrection — in which life there lies the real, actual, and final good. In this rests all the power and work of Christ, in this lies his real love toward us and our love toward him; whereas all the other things are only the condition, the path, the preliminary steps. Without faith in the accomplished resurrection of One, and without cherishing the future resurrection of all, all talk of some Kingdom of God remains nothing but words while, in reality, one finds only the Kingdom of Death.

PRINCE – Why that?

MR. Z. – Why, because you not only admit with everybody else the *fact* of death as such, that is that people have generally died, die, and will die, but you raise this fact to the position of an absolute law which does not in your opinion permit of a single exception. But what should we call the world in which death forever has the force of an absolute law if not the Kingdom of Death? And what is your Kingdom of God on Earth but an arbitrary and purposeless euphemism for the Kingdom of Death?

POLITICIAN – I also think it is purposeless, because it is wrong to replace a known quantity by an unknown one. Nobody has seen God and nobody knows what his Kingdom may be. But we have all seen the death of people and animals, and we also know that nobody in the world can escape this supreme power of death. What is the good, then, of replacing this certain "a" by some unknown "x"? Nothing but confusion and temptation for the "little ones" will ever result from such a substitution.

PRINCE – I don't quite understand what it is that we are talking about. Death is, of course, a very interesting phenomenon. One may perhaps call it even a law, in the sense of a phenomenon which is universal among earthly beings and unavoidable for any one of them. One may also speak of the absoluteness of this "law," as until now no exception has been authentically recorded. But what material vital importance can all this have for the true Christian teaching which speaks to us, through our conscience, of only one thing: that is, what we must and what we must not do *here* and *now*? It is also obvious that the voice of conscience can refer only to what is in our power to do or not to do. For this reason, conscience not only remains silent about death but cannot be anything else. With all its vastness for our human, worldly feelings and desires, death is not controlled by our will and cannot, therefore, have any moral significance for us. In this relation — and, properly speaking, it is of course the only important one — death is a fact of indifference similar, say, to bad weather. Because I recognize the unavoidable periodical existence of bad weather and have to suffer from it to a greater or smaller extent, does it follow that for this reason I should, instead of speaking of the Kingdom of God, speak of the kingdom of bad weather?

MR. Z. – No, you should not; first, because it reigns only in St. Petersburg, and we both come here to the Mediterranean and laugh at it; and, second, your comparison is faulty because, even in bad weather, you are able to praise God and feel yourself in his Kingdom, while the dead, as you know from the Bible, do not praise God. I agree for these reasons with his Excellency that it is more appropriate to call this world the Kingdom of Death than the Kingdom of God.

LADY – Why are you arguing all the time about titles? It is so uninteresting. Titles, surely, matter very little. You had better tell me, Prince, what you actually understand by the Kingdom of God and his truth.

PRINCE – By this I understand the state of human beings when they act only in accordance with their inner conscience and thus carry out the will of God which prescribes them nothing but pure good.

MR. Z. – The voice of conscience, however, speaks of performing what is due only *now* and *here*. Isn't this the view you hold?

PRINCE – You are quite correct.

MR. Z. – But does your conscience remain silent about those wicked deeds that you may have committed in your youth in relation to people long since dead?

PRINCE – In such cases the meaning of such reminders would be to warn me against repeating similar deeds *now*.

MR. Z. – Well, not exactly. But we need not argue about it. I would only like to indicate another more incontestable limit of conscience. For a long time moralists have been comparing the voice of conscience with that genius or daimon which accompanied Socrates warning him against things he should not do but never giving a positive indication as to what he should do. Precisely the same may be said of conscience.

PRINCE – How is that? Does not conscience suggest to me, say, that I should help my neighbor in case of need or danger?

MR. Z. – I am very glad to hear this from you. But if you examine such cases thoroughly you will see that the *role* of conscience even here remains purely negative: it demands from you only that you should not remain inactive or indifferent in the face of your neighbor's need. But, as to what you should do and how, this your conscience does not disclose.

PRINCE – Naturally so, because it depends on the circumstances of the case, on my own situation, and that of the neighbor whom I must help.

MR. Z. – Just so. But weighing and appraising these circumstances is not a matter of conscience but of reason.

PRINCE – How can you separate reason from conscience?

MR. Z. – You need not separate them, but you must distinguish them because, in reality, it sometimes happens that reason and conscience become not only separated but even opposed to each other. Were they one and the same thing, how would it be possible for reason to be used for acts not only foreign to morality but positively immoral? And, you know, this does happen. Why, even help can be offered in a way that is approved by reason but is inimical to moral consciousness. For instance, I may give food and drink and show other consideration to a needy man in order only to make him an accomplice in a fraud I am preparing, or any other wicked act.

PRINCE – That is, of course, elementary. But what conclusion do you deduce from it?

MR. Z. – The conclusion I deduce is that, if the voice of conscience, however important it may be for the purpose of warning and reproving you, does not at the same time give you any positive and practical, definite instructions for your conduct; and if, further, our good will requires reason as a subsidiary instrument, whereas its services prove rather doubtful (as it is equally ready to serve two masters, namely, good and evil) it follows that, for carrying out the will of God and attaining to the Kingdom of God, a third thing is necessary besides conscience and reason.

PRINCE – And what is that?

MR. Z. – Briefly, it is the *inspiration of the good,* or the direct and positive action of the good power itself on and within us. With this help from above, both reason and conscience become trustworthy assistants of good. Morality itself, instead of the always doubtful "good conduct," is transformed into a real life in the good — into an organic growth and development of the whole person — of his internal and external self, of personality and of society, of nation and of humanity — in order to attain to the vital unity of the risen past with the evolving future in that eternal present of the Kingdom of God which will be, though on the earth, the new Earth, joined in love with the new Heaven.

PRINCE – I have nothing to say against such poetical metaphors but do not exactly see why people, performing the will of God according to the commandments laid down in the Gospel, lack what you call "the inspiration of good."

MR. Z. – I do not see in their actions any signs of such an inspiration of good. I do not see any signs of those free and seeping impulses of love (God does not measure out the spirit he gives). Nor do I see that joyous and compliant peace that arises from the possession of those gifts, even in an elementary form. But, chiefly, I presuppose in the people you speak of a lack of inspiration of good because, in your opinion, it is unnecessary. If good is confined only to carrying out the "rule," there is no room left for inspiration of any kind. A "rule" is given once and for all, is definite and the same for everyone. The one who gave the rule has been dead long since, and, according to you, never rose to life, so that he has no personal vital existence for us. At the same time, you see the absolute, primary good not as a father of light and life who could breathe light and life straight into you, but as a prudent lord who sent you, his hirelings, to do the work in his vineyard, while he himself lives somewhere abroad and sends his men to you to bring him his rent.

PRINCE – We did not invent that image arbitrarily.

MR. Z. – No, you did not, but you do arbitrarily see in it the highest standard of relations between a person and the Deity, arbitrarily casting out of the Gospel its most essential part, the reference to the son and heir, in which the true standard of relations between people and God is given. You speak of the lord, duties toward the lord, the will of the lord. But I will tell this much: so long as your lord only imposes duties on you and demands from you compliance with his will, I do not see how you can prove to me that he is a true lord and not an impostor.

PRINCE – This is very funny, really! But what if I know in my conscience and reason that the lord's demands express the purest good?

MR. Z. – Pardon me, I am not speaking about this. I do not deny that the lord demands good from you. But how does it follow that he is good himself?

PRINCE – What else could he be?

MR. Z. – How strange. I have always thought that the goodness of anyone is proved not by what one wants other people to do but by one's own acts. If this is not clear to you from the standpoint of logic, I will quote you an historical example. The Moscow Tsar, Ivan the Terrible, demanded in his well-known letter to Prince Andrey Kurbsky that the Prince show the greatest goodness, the loftiest moral heroism, by refusing to resist force and meekly accepting the death of a martyr for the cause of truth. This lord's will was a will of good as far as its demands on the other were concerned. However, this did not prove in the least that the lord who demanded that good was good himself. It is evident that though martyrdom for the cause of truth is of the highest moral value, this does not say anything for Ivan the Terrible as he, in that case, was not a martyr but a torturer.

PRINCE – Perhaps. But what do you want to prove by this?

MR. Z. – Simply that until you show me the goodness of your lord in his own deeds and not in verbal precepts to his employees, I shall stick to my opinion that your distant lord, demanding good from others but doing no good himself, imposing duties but showing no love, never appearing before your eyes but living *incognito* somewhere abroad, is no one else but *the god of this world.*

GENERAL – Here it is, this damned *incognito!*

LADY – No more of this, please. How frightful! The power of the Cross be with us! (*Crosses herself.*)

PRINCE – One might have expected this all along!

MR. Z. – I have no doubt, Prince, that you are genuinely erring when you take the clever impostor for the real God. The *cleverness* of the impostor is a mitigating circumstance which greatly reduces your own guilt. I myself could not immediately see through it. But now I have no doubts of any kind, so you will understand with what feeling I must look at what I consider a deceptive and seductive *mask* of the good.

LADY – How can you say this? It hurts one's feelings.

PRINCE – I can assure you, madam, it has not hurt mine. The question raised here is a general one, and it presents some considerable interest. It is only strange that my opponent seems to imagine that it can be addressed only to me and not to him as well. You demand of me that I show you the personal good deeds of my lord that would prove him to be a power of good and not of evil. Very well. But can you show any good deed of your lord which I should be unable to ascribe to mine?

GENERAL – You have already heard of one such deed by which all the rest stand.

PRINCE – What is it?

MR. Z. – The real victory over evil in the real resurrection. Only this, I repeat, opens the real Kingdom of God whereas, without it, you have only the kingdom of death and sin and their creator, the Devil. The resurrection, and not in its metaphorical, but in its literal meaning — here is the testimony of the true God.

PRINCE – Well, if you are pleased to believe in such mythology! But I asked you for facts, which could be proved and not for your beliefs.

MR. Z. – Not so fast, Prince, not so fast. We both start from the same belief, or mythology if you like, with this difference — that I consistently carry it through to its logical end; while you, violating logic, arbitrarily stop at the first stage. After all, you do recognize the power of good and its coming triumph over evil, don't you?

PRINCE – Most emphatically!

MR. Z. – But what is it: a fact or a belief?

PRINCE – A *reasonable* belief.

MR. Z. – Let us see if it is so. Reason, as we have been taught at school, among other things demands that nothing should be accepted without sufficient grounds. Now tell me what sufficient grounds have you, while admitting the power that good has in the moral development and perfection of human beings and humanity, not to admit that power against death?

PRINCE – In my opinion, it is for you to answer why you attribute to good some power beyond the limits of the moral sphere.

MR. Z. – Oh, I can answer that. If I believe in good and its own power, while assuming in the very notion of good its essential and *absolute* superiority, then I am bound *by logic* to recognize that power as unlimited, and nothing can prevent me from believing in the truth of resurrection which has been *historically* confirmed. Had you frankly told me from the beginning that Christian *faith* does not concern you, that the subject of it is only mythology for you, then I should naturally have refrained from that animosity to your ideas which I have been unable to conceal from you. For "fallacy and error are not debited as frauds," and to bear ill will to people because of their fallacious theoretical notions would disclose one as possessing too feeble a mind, too weak a faith, and too wretched a heart. But anyone who is really religious, and thereby freed from these extremes of stupidity, cowardice, and heartlessness, must look with real goodwill at a straightforward, frank, in a word, *honest* opponent and denier of religious truths. It is so rare to meet such a one in our time, and it is difficult for me to describe how pleased I am when I see an open enemy of Christianity. In nearly every one of them, I am almost inclined to see a future St. Paul, while every Christian zealot seems to be a potential Judas, the traitor himself. But you, Prince, have now stated your opinion so frankly that I positively refuse to include you among the innumerable male and female Judases of our time. I can even foresee the moment when I shall feel toward you the same kind disposition of humor which I experience when meeting out-and-out atheists and infidels.

POLITICIAN – Now that we have safely come to the conclusion that neither those atheists and infidels nor such "true" Christians as our Prince represent the Anti-Christ, it is time for you to show us his real portrait.

MR. Z. – You want rather too much, your Excellency. Are you satisfied, for instance, with a single one of all the innumerable portraits of Christ which, you will admit, have sometimes been made even by artists of genius? Personally, I don't know of a single satisfactory portrait. I believe such is even impossible, for Christ is an individual, unique in his own kind and in the personification of his essence — good. To paint his portait, a genius will not suffice. The same must be said of the Anti-Christ: he is also an individual, singular in completeness and finish, a personification of evil. It is impossible to show his portrait. In Church literature, we find only his passport with a general description and some special marks . . .

LADY – No; we do not want his portrait, God save us! You had better explain why he himself is necessary, what his mission is, and when he will come.

MR. Z. – Well, in this respect I can satisfy you even better than you expect. Some few years ago a fellow-student from the Church Academy, later made a monk, on his deathbed bequeathed to me a manuscript which he valued very much, but was unwilling and unable to publish. It was entitled, "*A Short Story of the Anti-Christ.*" Though dressed in the form of fiction, as an imaginary forecast of the historical future, this paper, in my opinion, gives all that could be said on this subject in accordance with the Bible, with Church tradition, and with the dictates of sound sense.

POLITICIAN – Is it the work of our old friend Monk Barsanophius?

MR. Z. – No; this one's name was even more exquisite: Pansophius he was called.

POLITICIAN – Pan Sophius? Was he a Pole?

MR. Z. – Not in the least. A son of a Russian parson. If you will permit me to go upstairs to my room I will fetch the manuscript and then read it to you.

LADY – Hurry! See that you don't get lost!

(While Mr. Z. was out, the company left their seats and walked in the garden.)

POLITICIAN – I wonder what it is. Is it my eyesight that is getting weak, or is something taking place in nature? I notice that in no season, in no place, does one see those bright clear days which formerly used to be met with in every climate. Take today: there is not a single cloud, and we are far from the sea, and yet everything seems to be tinged with something subtle and imperceptible which, though small, destroys the full clearness of things. Do you notice this, General?

GENERAL – It is many a year since I began to notice it.

LADY – Last year I also began to notice, and not only in the air, but in the soul as well, that even the "full clearness," as you style it, is no longer to be found. All is seized with some uneasiness and some ill-omened presentiment. I am sure, Prince, you feel it, too.

PRINCE – No; I haven't noticed anything particular: the air seems to be as usual.

GENERAL – You are still too young to notice the difference, for you have nothing to compare with. But, when one remembers the fifties, one begins to feel it.

PRINCE – I think the explanation first suggested was the correct one: it is a matter of weak eyesight.

POLITICIAN – It is hardly open to argument that we are always growing older. But neither is the earth getting younger, so that our mutual fatigue now begins to show itself.

GENERAL – I think it is even more likely that the Devil, with his tail, is spreading fog over the world. Another sign of the Anti-Christ!

LADY (*pointing to Mr. Z., who was coming down from the terrace*) – We shall soon learn something about this.

(*All took their seats, and Mr. Z. began to read his manuscript.*)

A Short Story of the Anti-Christ

Pan-Mongolism! The name is wild,
Yet it pleases my ear greatly,
As if it were full of forebodings
Of the glorious providence of God.

LADY – Where does this motto come from?

MR. Z. – I think it is the work of the author himself.

LADY – Well, we are listening.

MR. Z. (*reads*) – The twentieth century was the epoch of the last great wars and revolutions. The greatest of these wars had its distant cause in the movement of *Pan-Mongolism* which originated in Japan as far back as the end of the nineteenth century. The imitative Japanese, who showed such wonderful speed and success in copying the external forms of European culture, also assimilated certain European ideas of the baser sort. Having learned from newspapers and textbooks on history that there were in the

West such movements as Pan-Hellenism, Pan-Germanism, Pan-Slavism, and Pan-Islamism, they proclaimed to the world the great idea of Pan-Mongolism — the unification under their leadership of all the races of Eastern Asia, with the aim of conducting a decisive war against foreign intruders, that is, against the Europeans. Taking advantage of the fact that at the beginning of the twentieth century Europe was engaged in a final decisive struggle against the *Moslem* world, they seized the opportunity to attempt the realization of their great plan — first, by occupying Korea, then Peking, where, assisted by the revolutionary party in China, they deposed the old Manchu dynasty and put in its place a Japanese one. In this the Chinese Conservatives soon acquiesced, as they understood that, of two evils, the lesser is the better, and that "family ties make all people brothers, whether they wish it or not." The independence of old China as a *state* had already proved unable to maintain itself, and subjection to the Europeans or the Japanese became inevitable. It seemed clear that the dominance of the Japanese, though it abolished the external forms of the Chinese state organization (which anyway had become palpably worthless), would not interfere with the main foundations of national life, whereas the dominance of the European Powers, which for political reasons supported the Christian missionaries, threatened the very spiritual basis of China. The national hatred in which the Japanese were formerly held by the Chinese had developed at a time when neither one nor the other knew the Europeans, and consequently this enmity of two kindred nations acquired the character of a family feud and was as unreasonable as it was ridiculous. The Europeans, however, were *unreservedly* alien, *nothing but* enemies, and their predominance promised nothing that could flatter national ambition, while in the hands of Japan the Chinese saw the delightful lure of Pan-Mongolism which, at the same time, was more acceptable to their minds than the painful necessity of assimilating the external forms of the European culture.

"Will you understand, you obstinate brothers," the Japanese repeatedly urged them, "that we take weapons from the Western dogs, not because we like them, but simply to beat them with their own devices? If you join us and accept our practical guidance, we shall soon be able not only to drive out all the white devils from our Asia but, also, to conquer their own lands and establish the true Middle Kingdom over the whole world. You are right in your national pride and your contempt for the Europeans but you should nourish these feelings, not only with dreams but with sensible actions as well. In these latter, we Japanese are far in advance of you and have to show you the ways of mutual benefit. If you look around, you will see yourselves what little gains you have obtained by your policy of confidence in yourselves and mistrust of us, your natural friends and protectors. You have seen how Russia and England, Germany and France nearly divided you up among themselves, and how all your tigerish schemes could show only the harmless end of the serpent's tail." The sensible Chinese found this argument reasonable, and the Japanese dynasty became firmly established. Its first care was, of course, to create a powerful army and fleet. The greater part of the Japanese troops were brought over to China and served as a nucleus for the new colossal army. The Japanese officers who could speak Chinese proved much more successful instructors than the dismissed Europeans, while the immense population of China, with Manchuria, Mongolia, and Tibet, provided a sufficient supply of good fighting material. It was already possible for the first Emperor of the Japanese dynasty to make a successful test of the power of the new Empire by driving out the French from Tonkin and Siam, the English from Burma, and then by adding the whole of Indochina to the Middle Kingdom. His successor, the second Emperor, Chinese on his mother's side, combined in himself Chinese cunning and tenacity with Japanese energy, agility, and enterprise. He mobilized an army four million strong in Chinese Turkestan, and while

Tsun-li-Yamin was confidentially informing the Russian Ambassador that this army was intended for the invasion of India, the Emperor with his immense forces suddenly invaded Russian Central Asia. Here, having raised against us all the population, he rapidly crossed the Ural Mountains, overrunning Eastern and Central Russia with his troops. Meanwhile, the Russian armies, mobilized in all haste, were hurrying to meet them from Poland and Lithuania, Kiev and Volhyn, St. Petersburg, and Finland. Having no ready plan of campaign, and being faced with an immense superiority in numbers, the fighting qualities of the Russian armies were sufficient only to allow them to perish with honor. The swiftness of the invasion left them no time for a proper concentration, and army corps after army corps were annihilated in desperate and hopeless battles. The Mongolian victories also involved huge losses, but these were easily made good with the help of the many Asiatic railways, while the Russian army, two hundred thousand strong and for some time concentrated on the Manchurian frontier, made an abortive attempt to invade well-defended China. After leaving a portion of his forces in Russia, so that no new armies could form in that country — and also in order to fight the numerous bodies of partisan units — the Emperor crossed the frontiers of Germany with three armies. In this case the country had had sufficient time to prepare itself, and one of the Mongolian armies met with a crushing defeat. At this time, the party of a belated *revanche* was in power in France, and soon the Germans found an army of a million bayonets in their rear. Finding itself between the hammer and the anvil, the German army was compelled to accept the honorable terms of peace offered to it by the Chinese Emperor. The exultant French, fraternizing with the yellow faces, scattered over Germany and soon lost all notion of military discipline. The Emperor ordered his army to kill any allies who were no longer useful and, with Chinese punctiliousness, the order was executed with precision. Simultaneously, in Paris, workers *sans patrie* organized an uprising and the capital of Western culture joyfully opened its gates to the Lord of the East. His curiosity satisfied, the Emperor set off to Boulogne where, protected by the fleet that had come round from the Pacific, transports were speedily prepared for ferrying his army over to England. The Emperor was in need of money, however, and so the English succeeded in buying him off with the sum of one million pounds. Within a year, all the European States submitted as vassals to the domination of the Chinese Emperor, who, having left sufficient occupation troops in Europe, returned to the East in order to organize naval expeditions against America and Australia.

The new Mongolian yoke over Europe lasted for half a century. The domain of the inner life of thought of this epoch was marked by a general blending and mutual interchange of European and Eastern ideas, providing a repetition on a grand scale of ancient Alexandrian syncretism. In the practical domain, three phenomena above all were most characteristic: the great influx into Europe of Chinese and Japanese workers and the consequent acuteness of social and economic problems; the continued activity of the ruling classes in the way of palliative attempts in order to solve those problems; and, lastly, the increased activity of secret international societies, organizing a great European conspiracy for expelling the Mongols and reestablishing the independence of Europe. This colossal conspiracy, which was supported by local national governments, insofar as they could evade the control of the Emperor's viceroys, was organized in masterly fashion and was crowned with most brilliant success. An appointed hour saw the beginning of a massacre of the Mongolian soldiers and of the annihilation and expulsion of the Asiatic workers. Secret cadres of European troops were suddenly revealed in various places, and a general mobilization was carried out according to plans previously prepared. The new Emperor, who was a grandson of the great conqueror, rushed from China to Russia, but his innumerable

hordes suffered a crushing defeat at the hands of the
All-European Army. Their scattered remnants returned to
the interior of Asia, and Europe breathed freely again. If the
half-century of submission to the Asiatic barbarians was due
to the disunity of the European States which had concerned
themselves only with their own national interests, a great
and glorious independence was achieved by an international
organization of the united forces of the entire European
population. As a natural consequence of this fact, the old
traditional organization of individual States was everywhere
deprived of its former importance, and the last traces of
ancient monarchal institutions gradually disappeared. Europe in the twenty-first century represented an alliance of
more or less democratic nations — the United States of
Europe. The progress of material culture, somewhat interrupted by the Mongolian yoke and the war of liberation, now
burst forth with a greater force. The problems of inner
consciousness, however, such as the questions of life and
death, the ultimate destiny of the world and humanity, made
more complicated and involved by the latest researches and
discoveries in the fields of psychology and physiology —
these as before remained unsolved. Only one important,
though negative, result made itself apparent. This was the
final bankruptcy of the materialistic theory. The notion of the
universe as a system of dancing atoms, and of life as the
result of mechanical accumulation of the slightest changes in
material no longer satisfied a single reasoning intellect.
Humanity had outgrown that stage of philosophical infancy.
On the other hand, it became equally evident that it had also
outgrown the infantile capacity for naive, unconscious faith.
Such ideas as God *creating* the universe *out of nothing* were no
longer taught even in elementary schools. A certain high
level of ideas concerning such subjects had been evolved,
and no dogmatism could risk a descent below it. And though
the majority of thinking people had remained faithless, the
few believers, of necessity, had become *thinking*, thus fulfill-

ing the commandment of the Apostle: "Be infants in your hearts, but not in your reason."

At that time, there was among the few believing spiritualists a remarkable person — many called him a superman —who was equally far from both, intellect and childlike heart. He was still young, but owing to his great genius, by the age of thirty-three he had already become famous as a great thinker, writer, and public figure. Conscious of the great power of spirit in himself, he was always a confirmed spiritualist, and his clear intellect always showed him the truth of what one should believe in: the good, God, and the Messiah. In these he *believed*, but he *loved* only *himself*. He believed in God, but in the depths of his soul he involuntarily and unconsciously preferred himself. He believed in Good, but the All Seeing Eye of the Eternal knew that this man would bow down before the power of Evil as soon as it would offer him a bribe — not by deception of the senses and the lower passions, not even by the superior bait of power, but only by his own immeasurable self-love. This self-love was neither an unconscious instinct nor an insane ambition, Apart from his exceptional genius, beauty, and nobility of character, the reserve, disinterestedness, and active sympathy with those in need which he evinced to such a great extent seemed abundantly to justify the immense self-love of this great spiritualist, ascetic, and philanthropist. Did he deserve blame because, being as he was so generously supplied with the gifts of God, he saw in them the signs of Heaven's special benevolence to him, and thought himself to be second only to God himself? In a word, he considered himself to be what Christ in reality was. But this conception of his higher value showed itself in practice not in the exercise of his moral duty to God and the world but in seizing his privilege and advantage at the expense of others, and of Christ in particular.

At first, he bore no ill feeling toward Christ. He recognized his messianic importance and value, but he was sincere in seeing in him only his own greatest precursor. The moral achievement of Christ and his uniqueness were beyond an intellect so completely clouded by self-love as his. Thus he reasoned: "Christ came before me. I come second. But what, in order of time, appears later is, in its essence, of greater importance. I come last, at the end of history, and for the very reason that I am most perfect. I am the final savior of the world, and Christ is my precursor. His mission was to precede and prepare for my coming." Thinking thus, the superman of the twenty-first century applied to himself everything that was said in the Gospels about the second coming, explaining the latter not as a return of the same Christ, but as a replacing of the preliminary Christ by the final one — that is, by himself.

At this stage, the coming man presented few original characteristics or features. His attitude toward Christ resembled, for instance, that of Mohammed, a truthful man, against whom no charge of harboring evil designs can be brought.

This man justified his selfish preference of himself before Christ in yet another way. "Christ," he said, "who preached and practiced moral good in life, was a *reformer* of humanity, whereas I am called to be the *benefactor* of that same humanity, partly reformed and partly incapable of being reformed. I will give everyone what they require. As a moralist, Christ divided humanity by the notion of good and evil. I shall unite it by benefits which are as much needed by good as by evil people. I shall be the true representative of that God who makes his sun to shine upon the good and the evil alike, and who makes the rain to fall upon the just and the unjust. Christ brought the sword; I shall bring peace. Christ threatened the earth with the Day of Judgment. But I shall be the last judge, and my judgment will be not only that of justice but also that of mercy. The justice that will be meted out in my sentences will not be a retributive justice but a distributive one. I shall judge each person according to his deserts, and shall give everybody what he needs."

In this magnificent spirit he now waited for God to call him in some unmistakable way to take upon himself the work of saving humanity — for some obvious and striking testimony that he was the elder son, the beloved first-born child of God. He waited and sustained himself by the consciousness of his superhuman virtues and gifts, for, as was said, he was a man of irreproachable morals and exceptional genius.

Thus this just, proud man awaited the sanction of the Most High in order to begin his saving of humanity; but he saw no signs of it. He had passed the age of thirty. Three more years passed. Suddenly, a thought leaped into his mind and thrilled him to the core. "What," he thought, "what if by some accident it is not I, but the other . . . the Galilean. What if he is not my annunciator but the true deliverer, the first and the last? In that case, he must be *alive* . . . But where is he, then? What if he suddenly comes to me . . . here, now? What shall I tell Him? Shall I not be compelled to kneel down before him as the very last silly Christian, as some Russian peasant who mutters without understanding: 'Lord, Jesus Christ, forgive me, a sinful man'? Shall I not be compelled like an old Polish woman to prostrate myself? I, the serene genius, the superman! It cannot be!" And here, instead of his former reasoning and cold reverence to God and Christ, a sudden fear was born and grew in his heart, next followed by a burning *envy* that consumed all his being, and by an ardent hatred that took his very breath away. "It is I, it is I, and not he! He is dead — is and will ever be! He did not — no, did not rise! He is rotting in the grave, rotting as the lost . . ." His mouth foaming, he rushed convulsively out of the house, through the garden, and ran along a rocky path into the silent black night.

His rage calmed down and gave place to a despair, dry and heavy as the rocks, somber as the night. He stopped in front of a sharp precipice, from the bottom of which he could hear the faint sounds of the stream running over the stones. An unbearable anguish pressed upon his heart. Suddenly a thought flashed across his mind. "Shall I call him? Shall I ask him what to do?" And in the midst of darkness he could see a pale and grief-stained image. "He pities me . . . Oh, no, never! He did not rise! He did not! He did not!" And he leapt from the precipice. But something firm like a column of water held him up in the air. He felt a shock as if of electricity, and some unknown force hurled him back. For a moment he became unconscious. When he came to his senses he found himself kneeling down a few paces from the brow of the precipice. A strange figure gleaming with a dim phosphorescent light loomed up before him, and its two eyes pierced his soul with their painful penetrating glitter . . .

He saw these two piercing eyes and heard some unfamiliar voice coming from inside or outside him — he could not tell which — a dull, muffled voice, yet distinct, metallic, and expressionless as a recording. And the voice said to him: "Oh, my beloved son! Let all my benevolence rest on thee! Why didst not thou seek for me? Why hast thou stooped to worship that other, the bad one, and his father? I am thy god and father. And that crucified beggar — he is a stranger both to me and to thee. I have no other son but thee. Thou art the sole, the only begotten, the equal of myself. I love thee, and ask for nothing from thee. Thou art so beautiful, great, and mighty. Do thy work in *thine own* name, not mine. I harbor no envy of thee. I love thee. I require nothing of thee. He whom thou regardest as God, demanded of his son obedience, absolute obedience — even to death on a cross — and even there he did not help Him. I demand nothing of thee, and I will help thee. For the sake of thyself, for the sake of thine own dignity and excellency, and for the sake of my own disinterested love of thee, I will help thee! Receive thou my spirit! As before my spirit gave birth to thee in *beauty*, so now it gives birth to thee in *power*." With these words, the superman's mouth opened involuntarily, two piercing eyes came close to his face, and he felt an icy breath which pervaded the whole of his being. He felt in himself such strength, vigor, lightness, and joy as he had never before experienced. At that moment, the luminous image and the two eyes suddenly disappeared, and something lifted the man into the air and brought him down in his own garden before the very doors of his house.

Next day, the visitors of the great man, and even his servants, were startled by his special inspired air. They would have been even more startled could they have seen with what supernatural quickness and facility he was writing, locked up in his study, his famous work entitled *The Open Way to Universal Peace and Prosperity.*

The superman's previous books and public activity had always met with severe criticism, though these came chiefly from people of exceptionally deep religious convictions, who for that very reason possessed no authority (I am, after all, speaking of the coming of the Anti-Christ) and thus they were hardly listened to when they tried to point out, in everything that the "coming man" wrote or said, the signs of a quite exceptional and excessive self-love and conceit, and a complete absence of true simplicity, frankness, and sincerity.

But now, with his new book, he brought over to his side even some of his former critics and adversaries. This book, composed after the incident at the precipice, evinced a greater power of genius than he had ever shown before. It was a work that embraced everything and solved every problem. It united a noble respect for ancient traditions and symbols with a broad and daring radicalism in socio-political questions. It joined a boundless freedom of thought with the most profound appreciation for everything mystical. Absolute individualism stood side by side with an ardent zeal for the common good, and the highest idealism in guiding principles combined smoothly with a perfect definiteness in practical solutions for the necessities of life. And all this was blended and cemented with such artistic genius that every thinker and every man of action, however one-sided he might have been, could easily view and accept the whole from his particular individual standpoint without sacrificing anything to the *truth itself*, without actually rising above his *ego*, without *in reality* renouncing his one-sidedness, without correcting the inadequacy of his views and wishes, and without making up their deficiencies. This wonderful book was immediately translated into the languages of all the civilized nations, and many of the uncivilized ones as well. During the entire year thousands of newspapers in all parts of the world were filled with the publisher's advertisements and the critics' praises. Cheap editions with portraits of the author were sold in millions of copies, and all the civilized world — which now stood for nearly all the globe — resounded with the glory of the incomparable, the great, the only one! Nobody raised his voice against the book. On every side it was accepted by all as the revelation of the complete truth. In it, all the past was given such full and due justice, the present was appraised with such impartiality and catholicity, and the happiest future was described in such a convincing and practical manner that everybody could not help saying: "Here at last we have what we need. Here is the ideal, which is not a Utopia. Here is a scheme which is not a dream." And the wonderful author not only impressed all, but he was *agreeable* to all, so that the word of Christ was fulfilled: "I have come in the name of the Father, and you accept me not. *Another* will come in *his own* name — him you *will* accept." For it is necessary to be *agreeable* to be *accepted*.

It is true some pious people, while praising the book wholeheartedly, had been asking why the name of Christ was never mentioned in it; but other Christians had rejoined: "So much the better. Everything sacred has already been stained enough in past ages by every sort of unacknowledged zealot, and nowadays a deeply religious author must be extremely guarded in these matters. Since the book is imbued with the true Christian spirit of active love and all-embracing goodwill, what more do you want?" And everybody agreed.

Soon after the publication of "The Open Way," which made its author the most popular man ever to live on earth, an international constitutional congress of the United States of Europe was to be held in Berlin. This Union, founded after a series of international and civil wars which had been brought about by the liberation from the Mongolian yoke and had resulted in considerable alteration in the map of Europe, was now menaced with peril, not through conflicts of nations but through the internal strife between various political and social parties. The principal directors of European policy, who belonged to the powerful brotherhood of Freemasons, felt the lack of a common executive power. The European unity that had been obtained at so great a cost was every moment threatening to fall to pieces. There was no unanimity in the Union Council or *"Comité permanent universel,"* for not all the seats were in the hands of true Masons. The independent members of the Council were entering into separate agreements, and this state of affairs threatened another war. The "initiated" then decided to establish a one-man executive power endowed with some considerable authority. The principal candidate was the secret member of the Order — "the Coming Man." He was the only man with a great worldwide fame. Being by profession a learned artilleryman, and by his source of income a rich capitalist, he was on friendly terms with many in financial and military circles. In another, less enlightened time, there might have been held against him the fact of his extremely obscure origin. His mother, a lady of doubtful reputation, was very well known in both hemispheres, but the number of people who had grounds to consider him as their son was rather too great. These circumstances, however, could not carry any weight with an age that was so advanced as to be actually the last. "The Coming Man" was almost unanimously elected president of the United States of Europe for life. And when he appeared on the platform in all the glamor of youthful superhuman beauty and power and, with inspired eloquence, expounded his universal program, the assembly was carried away by the spell of his personality and, in an outburst of enthusiasm, decided, even without voting, to give him the highest honor and to elect him Roman Emperor.

The congress closed amid general rejoicing, and the great man who had been chosen published a manifesto which began with the words: "Nations of the World! I give you my peace," and concluded, "Nations of the World! The promises have been fulfilled! An eternal universal peace has been secured. Every attempt to destroy it will meet with determined and irresistible opposition, since a middle power is now established on earth which is stronger than all the other powers, separately or conjointly. This unconquerable, all-surmountable power belongs to me, the authorized chosen one of Europe, the Emperor of all its forces. International law has at last secured the sanction which was so long missing. Henceforth, no country will dare to say 'War' when I say 'Peace!' Peoples of the world, peace to you!" This manifesto had the desired effect. Everywhere outside Europe, particularly in America, powerful imperialist parties were formed which compelled their governments to join the United States of Europe under the supreme authority of the Roman Emperor. There still remained a few independent tribes and little states in remote parts of Asia and Africa but, with a small but chosen army of Russian, German, Polish, Hungarian, and Turkish regiments, the Emperor set out for a military march from East Asia to Morocco and, without much bloodshed, brought into subjection all the insubordinate States. In all the countries of the two hemispheres, he installed his viceroys, choosing them from among the native nobility who had received a European education and were faithful to him. In all the heathen countries, the native populations, greatly impressed and charmed by his personality, proclaimed him as their supreme god. In a single year, a real universal monarchy in the true and proper sense of the word was established. The germs of wars were radically destroyed. The Universal League of Peace met for the last time, and having delivered an exalted panegyric to the Great Peacemaker, dissolved itself as being no longer necessary. On the eve of the second year of his reign, the World's Emperor published a new manifesto: "Nations of the World! I have promised you peace, and I have given it to you. But peace is joyful only through prosperity. Who in peacetime is threatened with poverty has no pleasure in peace. I call, therefore, all the cold and hungry ones to come to me, and I will give you food and warmth!" Here he announced the simple and comprehensive program of social reform that had already been articulated in his book and which now captured all noble and sound minds. Owing to the concentration in his hands of all the financial resources of the world and all its colossal land properties, the Emperor could carry into effect his reform in accordance with the wishes of the poor and without causing much pain to the rich. All now received according to their capabilities, and every capability according to its labors and merits.

The new lord of the world was above all else a kindhearted philanthropist and not only a philanthropist, but even a *philozoist*, a lover of life. He was a vegetarian himself, prohibited vivisection, and instituted strict supervision over the slaughter-houses; while societies for the protection of animals received from him every encouragement. But what was more important than these details, the most fundamental form of equality was firmly established among humankind, the *equality of universal satiety*. This took place in the second year of his reign. Social and economic problems finally had been settled. But if satisfaction is a question of primary importance for the hungry, the satisfied ones crave for something else. Even satiated animals usually want not only to sleep but also to play — the more so with humanity which has always *post panem* craved for *circenses*.

The Emperor Superman understood what his mob wanted. At that time a great magician, enwrapped in a dense cloud of strange facts and wild stories, came to him in Rome from the Far East. A rumor, spreading among the neo-Buddhists, credited him with a divine origin from the sun god Suria and some river nymph.

This magician, Apollonius by name, was doubtless a person of genius. A semi-Asiatic and a semi-European, a Catholic bishop *in partibus infidelium*, he combined in himself in a most striking manner knowledge of the latest conclusions and applications of Western science with the art of utilizing all that was really sound and important in traditional Eastern mysticism. The results of this combination were startling. Apollonius learned, among other things, the semiscientific, semi-mystic art of attracting and directing at will atmospheric electricity, and the people said of him that he could *bring down fire from heaven*. However, though he was able to startle the imagination of the crowd by various unheard-of phenomena, for some time he did not abuse his power for any special or selfish ends.

It was this man who came to the great Emperor, saluted him as the true son of God, declaring that he had discovered in the secret books of the East certain unmistakable prophecies pointing to the Emperor as the last savior and judge of the Universe, and offering him his services and all his art. The Emperor, completely charmed by the man, accepted him as a gift from above, decorated him with all kinds of gorgeous titles, and made him his constant companion. So the nations of the world, after they had received from their lord universal peace and universal abolition of hunger, were now given the possibility of never-ending enjoyment of most diverse and extraordinary miracles. Thus came to end the third year of the reign of the superman.

After this happy solution of political and social problems, the religious question came to the fore. The question was raised by the Emperor himself, in the first place, in its application to Christianity. At the time, the situation of Christianity was as follows: Its followers had greatly diminished in numbers and barely included forty-five million people in the whole world; but, morally, it had made a marked progress and had gained in quality what it had lost in numbers. People who were not bound to Christianity by any spiritual tie were no longer counted as Christians. The various Christian persuasions had diminished fairly equally in their numbers, so that the proportional relationship among them remained almost unchanged. As to mutual feelings, hostility had not entirely given place to amity but had considerably softened down, and points of disagreement had lost much of their former acuteness. The Papacy had long before been expelled from Rome, and after long wanderings had found refuge in St. Petersburg on condition that it refrain from propaganda there and in the country. In Russia, the Papacy soon became greatly simplified. Leaving practically unchanged the number of its colleges and offices, it was obliged to infuse into their work a more fervent spirit, and to reduce to the smallest limits its elaborate rituals and ceremonials. Many strange and seductive customs, though not formally abolished, fell of themselves into disuse. In all the other countries, particularly in North America, the Catholic priesthood still had a good many representatives possessed of strong will, inexhaustible energy, and independent character, who welded together the Catholic Church into a closer unity than it had ever seen before, and who preserved for it its international, cosmopolitan importance. As to Protestantism, which was still led by Germany, especially since the union of the greater part of the Anglican Church with the Catholic one — Protestantism had purged itself of its extreme negative tendencies, and the supporters of these tendencies openly descended into religious apathy and unbelief. The Evangelical Church now contained only the sincerely religious. It was headed by people who combined a vast learning with a deep religious feeling and an ever-growing desire to bring to life again in their own persons the living image of the true ancient Christianity. Russian Orthodoxy, after political events had altered the official position of the Church, lost many millions of its sham and nominal members; but it won the joy of unification with the best part of the "old believers," and even many of the deeply religious sectarians. The revivified Church, though not increasing in numbers, began to grow in strength of spirit, which it particularly revealed in its struggle with the numerous extremist sects (some not entirely devoid of the demoniacal and satanic element) which found root among the people and in society.

During the first two years of the new reign, all Christians, frightened and weary of the number of preceding revolutions and wars, looked upon their new lord and his peaceful reforms partly with benevolent expectation and partly with unreserved sympathy and even fervent enthusiasm. But in the third year, after the great magician had made his appearance, serious fears and antipathy began to grow in the minds of many an Orthodox, Catholic and Protestant. The Gospel and Apostolic texts speaking of the Prince of this Age and of the Anti-Christ were now read more carefully and led to lively comments. The Emperor soon perceived from certain signs that a storm was brewing, and he resolved to bring the matter to a head without any further delay. In the beginning of the fourth year of his reign, he published a manifesto to all true Christians, without distinction of churches, inviting them to elect or appoint authoritative representatives for the world congress to be held under his presidency. At that time, the imperial residence was transferred from Rome to Jerusalem. Palestine was already an autonomous province, inhabited and governed mainly by the Jews. Jerusalem was a free and now imperial city. The Christian shrines remained unmolested but, over the whole of the large platform of Haram-esh-Sheriff, extending from Birket-Israin and the barracks right to the mosque of El-Ax and "Solomon's Stables," an immense building was erected, incorporating in itself, besides the two small ancient mosques, a huge "Empire" temple for the unification of all cults, and two luxurious imperial palaces with libraries, museums, and special apartments for magical experiments and exercises. It was in this half-temple, half-palace that the world congress was to meet on September 14. As the Evangelical Church has no hierarchy in the proper sense of the word, the Catholic and Orthodox hierarchy, in compliance with the express wish of the Emperor, and in order that a greater uniformity of representation should obtain, decided to admit to the proceedings of the congress a certain number of lay members known for their piety and devotion to Church interests. Once, however, these were admitted, it seemed impossible to exclude from the congress the clergy, of both monastic and secular orders. In this way the total number of members at the congress exceeded three thousand, while about half a million Christian pilgrims flooded Jerusalem and all Palestine. Among the members present, three men were particularly conspicuous. The first was Pope Peter II, who legitimately led the Catholic part of the congress. His predecessor had died on the way to the congress, and a conclave had met in Damascus, and unanimously elected Cardinal Simone Barionini, who took the name of Peter. He came of plebeian stock, from the province of Naples, and had become famous as a preacher of the Carmelite Order, having earned great successes in fighting a certain Satanic sect which was spreading in St. Petersburg and its environs and seducing not only the Orthodox but the Catholic faithful as well. Raised to the archbishopric of Mogilov and next to the Cardinal's chair, he was all along marked for the tiara. He was a man of fifty, of middle stature and strongly built, with a red face, a crooked nose, and thick eyebrows. He had an impulsive and ardent temperament, spoke with fervor and with sweeping gestures, and enthused more than convinced his audience. The new Pope had no trust in the Emperor, and looked at him with a disapproving eye, particularly since the deceased Pope, yielding to the Emperor's pressure, had made a cardinal of the Imperial Chancellor and great magician of the world, the exotic Bishop Apollonius, whom Peter regarded as a doubtful Catholic and a certain fraud. The actual, though not official, leader of the Orthodox members was the Elder John, extremely well known among the Russian people. Officially, he was considered a bishop "in retirement," but he did not live in any monastery, being always engaged in travelling all over the world. Many legendary stories were circulated about him. Some people believed that he was Feodor Kuzmich, that is, Emperor Alexander I, who had died three centuries back and was now raised to life. Others went further and maintained that he was the true Elder John, that is, John the Apostle, who had never died and had now openly reappeared in the latter days. He himself said nothing about his origin and younger days. He was now a very old but vigorous man with white hair and a beard tinged with a yellowish, even greenish color, tall, thin in body, with full, slightly rosy cheeks, vivid sparkling eyes and a tender, kind expression in his face and speech. He was always dressed in a white cassock and mantle. Heading the Evangelical members of the congress was the very learned German theologian, Professor Ernst Pauli. He was a short, wizened old man, with a huge forehead, sharp nose, and a cleanly shaven chin. His eyes were distinguished by their peculiarly ferocious and yet kindly gaze. He incessantly rubbed his hands, shook his head, sternly knitted his brows and pursed up his lips; while with eyes all flashing he sternly ejaculated: "So! Nun! Ja! So also!" His dress bore all the appearance of solemnity — a white tie and long pastoral frock coat decorated with signs of his order.

The opening of the congress was most imposing. Two-thirds of the immense temple, devoted to the "unification of all cults," was covered with benches and other seating arrangements for members of the congress. The remaining third was taken up by a high platform on which were placed the Emperor's throne and another, lesser throne a little below it intended for the great magician — who was at the same time cardinal and imperial chancellor — and behind them rows of armchairs for the ministers, courtiers, and State officials, while along the side there were still longer rows of armchairs, the intended occupants of which remained undisclosed. The gallery was taken by the orchestra, while in the adjoining square there were installed two regiments of Guards and a battery of guns for triumphal salvos. The members of the congress had already attended their respective services in their various churches: the opening of the congress was to be entirely civil. When the Emperor, accompanied by the great magician and his suite, made his entrance, the band began to play the "March of Unified Humanity," which was the international hymn of the Empire, and all the members rose to their feet, and, waving their hats, gave three enthusiastic cheers: "Vivat! Hurrah! Hoch!" The Emperor, standing by the throne and stretching forward his hand with an air of majestic benevolence, proclaimed in a sonorous and pleasing voice: "Christians of all sects! My beloved subjects, brothers and sisters! From the beginning of my reign, which the Most High blessed with such wonderful and glorious deeds, I have had no cause to be dissatisfied with you. You have always performed your duties true to your faith and conscience. But this is not enough for me. My sincere love for you, my beloved brothers and sisters, thirsts for reciprocation. I wish you to recognize in me your true leader in every enterprise undertaken for the well-being of humanity, not merely out of your sense of duty to me but mainly out of your heartfelt love for me. So now, besides what I generally do for all, I am about to show you my special benevolence. Christians! What can I bestow upon you? What can I give you, not as my subjects, but as my coreligionists, my brothers and sisters! Christians! Tell me what is the most precious thing for you in Christianity, so that I may direct my efforts to that end?" He stopped for a moment, waiting for an answer. The hall was filled with reverberating muffled sounds. The members of the congress were consulting each other. Pope Peter, with fervent gestures, was explaining something to his followers. Professor Pauli was shaking his head and ferociously smacking his lips. The Elder John, bending over Eastern bishops and monks, quietly tried to impress something upon them. After he had waited a few minutes, the Emperor again addressed the congress in the same kind tone, in which, however, there could be heard a scarcely perceptible note of irony: "Dear Christians," he said, "I understand how difficult it is for you to give me a direct answer. I will help you also in this. From time immemorial, you have had the misfortune to have been broken up into various confessions and sects, so that now you have scarcely one common object of desire. But where you cannot agree among yourselves, I hope I shall be able to bring agreement to you by bestowing upon all your sects the same love and the same readiness to satisfy the *true desire* of each. Dear Christians! I know that for many, and not the least among you, the most precious thing in Christianity is the *spiritual authority* with which it endows its legal representatives — of course, not for their personal benefit, but for the common good, since on this authority firmly rests the true spiritual order and moral discipline so necessary for everyone. Dear brother Catholics, sister Catholics! How well I understand your view, and how much I would like to base my imperial power on the authority of your spiritual Head! In order that you should not think that this is mere flattery and windy words I, therefore, most solemnly declare that it is pleasing to our autocratic power that the Supreme Bishop of all Catholics, the Pope of Rome, be henceforth restored to his throne in Rome with all former rights and privileges belonging to this title and chair given at any time by our predecessors, from Constantine the Great onward. In return for this, Catholic brothers and sisters, I wish to receive from you only your inner heartfelt recognition of myself as your sole protector and patron. Let those here who recognize me in their hearts and consciences as their sole protector and patron come up to this side!" Here he pointed to the empty seats on the platform. And instantly, nearly all the princes of the Catholic Church, cardinals and bishops, the greater part of the laypeople and over half the monks, shouting in exultation "Gratias agimus! Domine! Salvum fac magnum imperatorem!" rose to the platform and, humbly bowing their heads to the Emperor, took their seats. Below, however, in the middle of the hall, straight and immovable, like a marble statue, still in his seat sat Pope Peter II. All those who had surrounded him were now on the platform. But the diminished crowd of monks and laypeople who remained below moved nearer and closed in a dense crowd around him. And one could hear the subdued mutter issuing from them: "Non praevalebunt, non praevalebunt portae inferni."

With a startled look cast at the immovable Pope, the Emperor again raised his voice: "Dear brothers and sisters! I know that there are among you many for whom the most precious thing in Christianity is its *sacred tradition* — the old symbols, the old hymns and prayers, the icons and the old rituals. What, indeed, could be more precious for a religious soul? Know, then, my beloved, that today I have signed the decree and have set aside vast sums of money for the establishment of a world museum of Christian archaeology in our glorious imperial city, Constantinople.

This museum shall have the aim of collecting, studying, and saving all the monuments of church antiquity, more particularly Eastern church antiquity; and I ask you to select tomorrow from your midst a committee for working out with me the measures which are to be carried out, so that modern life, morals, and customs may be organized as nearly as possible in accordance with the traditions and institutions of the Holy Orthodox Church. My Orthodox brothers and sisters! Those of you who view with favor this will of mine, who can in their inner consciousness call me their true leader and lord, let those come up here." Here the greater part of the hierarchy of the East and North, half of the former old believers and more than half of the Orthodox clergy, monks, and laypeople rose with joyful exclamation to the platform, casting suspicious eyes at the Catholics, who were already proudly occupying their seats. But the Elder John remained in his place, and sighed loudly. And when the crowd round him became greatly thinned, he left his bench and went over to Pope Peter and his group. He was followed by the other Orthodox members who did not go to the platform. Then the Emperor spoke again: "I am aware, dear Christians, that there are among you also such who place the greatest value upon personal assurance of the truth and the free examination of the Scriptures. There is no need for me to enlarge upon my views on this matter at the moment. Perhaps you are aware that, in my youth, I wrote a long treatise on biblical criticism which at that time excited much comment and laid the foundation for my popularity and reputation. In memory of this, I presume, the University of Tubingen only the other day requested me to accept the degree of a Doctor of Theology *honoris causa*. I have replied that I accept it with pleasure and gratitude. And today, simultaneously with the decree of the Museum of Christian Archaeology, I signed another decree establishing a world institute for the free examination of the sacred Scriptures from all points of

view and in all possible directions, and for study of all
subsidiary sciences — to which institute an annual sum of
one and one-half million marks is hereby granted. I call
those of you who look with sincere favor upon this act of
goodwill of mine and who are able in true feeling to
recognize me as their sovereign leader to come up here to
the new Doctor of Theology." A strange but hardly perceptible smile passed lightly over the beautiful lips of the great
man. More than half of the learned theologians moved to
the platform, though somewhat slowly and hesitatingly.
Everybody looked at Professor Pauli, who seemed to be
rooted to his seat. He dropped his head, bent down and
shrank. The learned theologians who had already managed
to get onto the platform seemed to feel very awkward, and
one of them even suddenly dropped his hand in renuncia-
tion, and, having jumped right down past the stairs, ran
hobbling to Professor Pauli and the members who remained with him. At this, the Professor raised his head,
rose to his feet as if without a definite objective in view, and
then walked past the empty benches, accompanied by
those among his coreligionists who had also withstood the
temptation. He took his seat near Elder John and Pope
Peter and their followers. The greater part of the members,
including nearly all the hierarchs of the East and West,
were now on the platform. Below there remained only
three groups of members, now coming more closely together and pressing around Elder John, Pope Peter, and
Professor Pauli.

Now, in a grieved voice, the Emperor addressed them:
"What else can I do for you, you strange people? What do
you want from me? I cannot understand. Tell me yourselves, you Christians, deserted by the majority of your
peers and leaders, condemned by popular sentiment. What
is it that you value most in Christianity?" At this, Elder
John rose up like a white candle and answered quietly:
"Great sovereign! What we value most in Christianity is

Christ himself — in his person. All comes from him, for we know that in him dwells all fullness of the Godhead bodily. We are ready, sire, to accept any gift from you, if only we recognize the holy hand of Christ in your generosity. Our candid answer to your question, what can you do for us, is this: Confess now and before us the name of Jesus Christ, the Son of God, who came in the flesh, rose, and who will come again — Confess his name, and we will accept you with love as the true forerunner of his second glorious coming." The Elder finished his speech and fixed his eyes on the face of the Emperor. A terrible change had come over it. A hellish storm was raging within him, like the one he experienced on that fateful night. He had completely lost his inner equilibrium, and was concentrating all his thoughts on preserving external control, so that he should not betray himself inopportunely. He was making a super-human effort not to throw himself with wild howls on Elder John and begin tearing him with his teeth. Suddenly, he heard a familiar, unearthly voice: "Be silent and fear not!" He remained silent. Only his face, livid like death, looked distorted and his eyes flashed. In the meantime, while Elder John was still making his speech, the great magician, wrapped in the ample tricolored mantle that covered nearly all his cardinal's purple, could be seen busily manipulating something concealed beneath it. The magician's eyes were fixed and flashing, and his lips moved slightly. Through the open windows of the temple an immense black cloud could be seen covering the sky. Soon, complete darkness set in. Elder John, startled and frightened, stared at the face of the silent Emperor. Suddenly, he sprang back and, turning to his followers, shouted in a stifled voice: "Little children, it is Anti-Christ!" At this moment, a great thunderbolt flashed into the temple, followed by a deafening thunderclap. It struck the Elder John. Everyone was stupefied for a second, and when the deafened Christians came to their senses, the Elder was seen lying dead on the floor.

The Emperor, pale but calm, addressed the assembly: "You have witnessed the judgment of God. I had no wish to take any man's life, but thus my Heavenly Father avenges his beloved son. It is finished. Who will oppose the will of the Most High? Secretaries, write this down: The Ecumenical Council of All Christians, after a foolish opponent of the Divine Majesty had been struck by fire from heaven, recognized unanimously the sovereign Emperor of Rome and all the Universe as its supreme leader and lord." Suddenly a word, loud and distinct, passed through the temple: "Contradicatur!" Pope Peter II rose. His face flushed, his body trembling with indignation, he raised his staff in the direction of the Emperor. "Our only Lord," he cried, "is Jesus Christ, the Son of the living God! And who you are, you have heard just now. Away! You Cain, you murderer! Get you gone, you incarnation of the Devil! By the authority of Christ, I, the servant of the servants of God, cast you out forever, foul dog, from the city of God, and deliver you up to your father Satan! Anathema! Anathema! Anathema!" While he was so speaking, the great magician was moving restlessly under his mantle. Louder than the last "Anathema!" the thunder rumbled, and the last Pope fell lifeless on the floor. "So die all my enemies by the arm of my Father!" cried the Emperor. "Pereant, pereant!" exclaimed the trembling princes of the Church. The Emperor turned and, supported by the great magician and accompanied by all his crowd, slowly walked out the door at the back of the platform. There remained in the temple only the corpses and a little knot of Christians half-dead from fear. The only person who did not lose control over himself was Professor Pauli. The general horror seemed to have raised in him all the powers of his spirit. He even changed in appearance; his countenance became noble and inspired. With determined steps, he walked up onto the platform, took one of the seats previously occupied by some State official, and began to write on a sheet of paper. When he had finished he rose and read in a loud voice: "To the glory of our only Savior, Jesus Christ! The Ecumenical Council of our Lord's churches, meeting in Jerusalem after our most blessed brother John, representative of Christianity in the East, had exposed the archdeceiver and enemy of God to be the true Anti-Christ foretold in Scripture; and after our most blessed father, Peter, representative of Christianity in the West, had lawfully and justly expelled him forever from the Church of God; now, before these two witnesses of Christ, murdered for the truth, this Council resolves: To cease all communion with the excommunicated one and with his abominable assembly, and to go to the desert and wait there for the inevitable coming of our true Lord, Jesus Christ." Enthusiasm seized the crowd, and loud exclamations could be heard on all sides. "Adveniat! Adveniat cito! Komm, Herr Jesu, komm! Come, Lord Jesus Christ!"

Professor Pauli wrote again and read: "Accepting unanimously this first and last deed of the last Ecumenical Council, we sign our names" — and here he invited those present to do so. All hurried to the platform and signed their names. And last on the list stood in big Gothic characters the signature: "Duorum defunctorum testium locum tenes Ernst Pauli." "Now let us go with our ark of the last covenant," he said, pointing to the two deceased. The corpses were put on stretchers. Slowly, singing Latin, German, and Church-Slavonic hymns, the Christians walked to the gate leading out from Haram-esh-Sheriff. Here the procession was stopped by one of the Emperor's officials who was accompanied by a squad of Guards. The soldiers remained at the entrance while the official read: "By order of his Divine Majesty. For the enlightenment of Christian people and for their protection from wicked people spreading unrest and temptation, we deem it necessary to resolve that the corpses of the two agitators, killed by heavenly fire, be publicly exhibited in the street of the

Christians (Haret-en-Nasara), at the entrance into the principal temple of this religion, called the Temple of our Lord's Sepulcher, or the Temple of the Resurrection, so that all may be persuaded of the reality of their death. Their obstinate followers, who wrathfully reject all our benefits and insanely shut their eyes to the patent signs of God himself are, by our mercy and presentation before our Heavenly Father, spared a much-deserved death by heavenly fire, and are left free with the sole prohibition, necessary for the common good, of not living in towns and other inhabited places of residence lest they disturb and tempt innocent, simpleminded folk with their malicious inventions." When the official had finished reading, eight soldiers, at a sign from the officer, approached the stretchers bearing the bodies.

"Let what is written be fulfilled," said Professor Pauli. And the Christians who were holding the stretchers silently passed them to the soldiers, who went away with them through the northwest gate. The Christians, having gone out through the northeast gate, hurriedly walked from the city past the Mount of Olives toward Jericho, along a road which had previously been cleared of other people by the gendarmes and two cavalry regiments. On the barren hills near Jericho, they decided to wait a few days. The following morning, friendly Christian pilgrims came from Jerusalem and told what had been going on in Zion. After the Court dinner, all the members of the congress were invited to a vast throne hall (near the supposed site of Solomon's throne), and the Emperor, addressing the representatives of the Catholic hierarchy, told them: that the well-being of their Church clearly demanded from them the immediate election of a worthy successor to the apostate Peter; that under the circumstances the election must needs be a summary one; that his, the Emperor's, presence as the leader and representative of the whole Christian world would amply make up for the inevitable omissions in the ritual; and that he, on behalf of all Christians, suggested that the Holy College elect his beloved friend and brother Apollonius, in order that their close friendship could unite Church and State firmly and indissolubly for their mutual benefit. The Holy College retired to a separate room for a conclave and, in an hour and a half, it returned with its new Pope, Apollonius. In the meantime, while the election was being carried out, the Emperor was meekly, sagaciously, and eloquently persuading the Orthodox and Evangelical representatives, in view of the new great era in Christian history, to put an end to their old dissensions, giving his word that Apollonius would be able to abolish all the abuses of the Papal authority known to history. Persuaded by this speech, the Orthodox and Protestant representatives drafted a deed of the unification of all churches, and when Apollonius appeared with the cardinals in the hall and was met by shouts of joy from all those present, a Greek bishop and an Evangelical pastor presented him with their document. "Accipio et approbo et laetificatur cor meum," said Apollonius, signing it. "I am as much a true Orthodox and a Protestant as I am a true Catholic," he added, and exchanged friendly kisses with the Greek and the German. Then he came up to the Emperor, who embraced him and long held him in his arms. At this time, tongues of flame began to dart about in the palace and the temple. They grew and became transformed into luminous shapes of strange beings and flowers never seen before came down from above, filling the air with an unknown perfume. Enchanting sounds of music, stirring the very depths of the soul, produced by unfamiliar instruments, were heard, while angelic voices of unseen singers sang the glory of the new lords of heaven and earth. Suddenly, a terrific subterranean noise was heard in the northwest corner of the palace under "Kubbet-el-Aruah," "the dome of souls," where, according to Muslim belief, the entrance to hell was hidden. When the assembly, invited by the

Emperor, went to that end, all could clearly hear innumerable voices, thin and penetrating — either childish or devilish — exclaiming: "The time has come, release us, dear saviors, dear saviors!" But when Apollonius, kneeling on the ground, shouted something downward in an unknown language three times, the voices died down and the subterranean noise subsided. Meanwhile, a vast crowd of people surrounded Haram-esh-Sheriff on all sides. Darkness set in and the Emperor, with the new Pope, came out upon the eastern terrace — the signal for "a storm of rejoicing." The Emperor bowed affably on all sides, while Apollonius took magnificent fireworks, rockets, and fountains from huge baskets brought up by the cardinal deacons. Igniting them by a mere touch of his hand, he tossed them one after another into the air where they glimmered like phosphorescent pearls and sparked with all the tints of a rainbow. Reaching the ground, all the sparkles transformed into numberless variously colored sheets containing complete and absolute indulgences of all sins — past, present, and future.[3] Popular exultation overflowed all limits. True, there were some who stated that they had seen with their own eyes the indulgences turn into hideous frogs and snakes. But the vast majority of the people were pleased immensely, and the popular festivities continued a few days longer. The prodigies of the new Pope now surpassed all imagination, so that it would be a hopeless task even to attempt a description of them. In the meantime, among the desert hills of Jericho, the Christians were devoting themselves to fasting and prayers.

On the evening of the fourth day, Professor Pauli and nine companions, mounted on asses and taking with them a cart, stole into Jerusalem and, passing through sidestreets by Haram-esh-Sheriff to Haret-en-Nasara, came to the entrance to the Temple of the Resurrection, in front of

---

[3] With reference to the above, see Preface. — Author.

which, on the pavement, the bodies of Pope Peter and Elder John were lying. The street was deserted at that time of night, as everyone had gone to Hasam-esh-Sheriff. The sentries were fast asleep. The party that came for the bodies found them quite untouched by decomposition, not even stiff or heavy. They put them on stretchers and covered them with the cloaks they had brought with them. Then by the same circuitous route they returned to their followers. They had hardly lowered the stretcher to the ground when suddenly the spirit of life could be seen reentering the deceased bodies. The bodies moved slightly as if they were trying to throw off the cloaks in which they were wrapped. With shouts of joy, everyone lent them aid and soon both the revived men rose to their feet, safe and sound. Then said Elder John: "Ah, my little children, we have not parted after all! I will tell you this: it is time that we carry out the last prayer of Christ for his disciples — that they should be all one, even as he himself is one with the Father. For this unity in Christ, let us honor our beloved brother Peter. Let him at last pasture the flocks of Christ. There it is, brother!" And he put his arms round Peter. Then Professor Pauli came nearer. "Tu est Petrus!" he said to the Pope, "*Jetzt ist es ja gründlich erwiesen und ausser jedem Zweifel gesetzt.*" And he shook Peter's hand firmly with his own right hand, while he stretched out his left hand to John saying: "*So also Väterchen nun sind wir ja Eins in Christo.*" In this manner, the unification of churches took place in the midst of a dark night on a high and deserted spot. But the nocturnal darkness was suddenly illuminated with brilliant light and a great sign appeared in the heavens; it was a woman, clothed in the sun with the moon beneath her feet and a wreath of twelve stars on her head. The apparition remained immovable for some time, and then began slowly to move in a southward direction. Pope Peter raised his staff and exclaimed: "Here is our banner! Let us follow it!" And he walked after that apparition, accompanied by both the old men and the whole crowd of Christians, to God's mountain, to Sinai . . .

(*Here the reader stopped.*)

LADY – Well, why don't you go on?

MR. Z. – The manuscript stops here. Father Pansophius could not finish his story. He told me when he was already ill that he thought of completing it "as soon as I get better," he said. But he did not get better, and the end of his story is buried with him in the graveyard of the Danilov Monastery.

LADY – But you remember what he told you, don't you? Please tell us.

MR. Z. – I remember it only in its main outlines. After the spiritual leaders and representatives of Christianity had departed to the Arabian desert, whither crowds of faithful believers of truth were streaming from all countries, the new Pope with his miracles and prodigies was able to corrupt unimpededly all the remaining, superficial Christians who were not yet disappointed with the Anti-Christ. He declared that by the power of his keys he could open the gates between the earthly world and the world beyond the grave. Communion of the living with the dead, and also of the living with demons, became a matter of everyday occurrence, and new unheard-of forms of mystic lust and demonolatry began to spread among the people. However, the Emperor had scarcely begun to feel himself firmly established on religious grounds, and, having yielded to the persistent suggestions of the seductive voice of the secret "father," had hardly declared himself the sole true incarnation of the supreme Deity of the Universe, when a new trouble came upon him from a side which nobody had expected: the Jews rose against him. This nation, whose numbers at that time had reached thirty million, was not altogether ignorant of the preparations for and the consolidation of the worldwide successes of the superman. When the Emperor transferred his residence to Jerusalem, secretly spreading among the Jews the rumor that his main object was to bring about a domination by Israel over the whole of the world, the Jews proclaimed him as their Messiah, and their exultation and devotion to him knew no bounds. But now they suddenly rose, full of wrath and thirsting for vengeance. This turn of events, doubtless foretold in both Gospel and church tradition, was pictured by Father Pansophius, perhaps, with too great a simplicity and realism. You see, the Jews, who regarded the Emperor as a true and perfect Israelite by blood, unexpectedly discovered that he was *not even circumcised*. The same day all Jerusalem, and next day all Palestine, were up in arms against him. The boundless and fervent devotion to the savior of Israel, the promised Messiah, gave place to as boundless and as fervent a hatred of the wily deceiver, the impudent impostor. The whole of the Jewish nation rose as one man, and its enemies were surprised to see that the soul of Israel at bottom lived not by calculations and aspirations of Mammon but by the power of an all-absorbing sentiment — the hope and strength of its eternal faith in the Messiah. The Emperor, taken by surprise at the sudden outburst, lost all self-control and issued a decree sentencing to death all insubordinate Jews and Christians. Many thousands and tens of thousands who could not arm themselves in time were ruthlessly massacred. But an army of Jews, one million strong, soon took Jerusalem and locked up the Anti-Christ in Haram-esh-Sheriff. His only support was a portion of the Guards who were not strong enough to overwhelm the masses of the enemy. Assisted by the magic art of his Pope, the Emperor succeeded in passing through the lines of his besiegers, and quickly appeared again in Syria with an innumerable army of pagans of different races. The Jews went forth to meet him with small hope of success. But hardly had the vanguard of both armies come together, when an earthquake of unprecedented violence occurred. An enormous volcano, with a giant crater, rose up by the Dead Sea, around which the imperial army was encamped. Streams of fire flowed together into a flaming lake that swallowed up the Emperor himself, together with his numberless forces — not to mention Pope Apollonius, who always accompanied him, and whose magic was of no avail. Meanwhile, the Jews hastened to Jerusalem in fear and trembling, calling for salvation to the God of Israel. When the Holy City was already in sight, the heavens were rent by vivid lightning from the east to the west, and they saw Christ coming toward them in royal apparel, and with the wounds from the nails in his outstretched hands. At the same time, the company of Christians led by Peter, John, and Paul came from Sinai to Zion, and from various other parts hurried more triumphant multitudes, consisting of all the Jews and Christians who had been killed by the Anti-Christ. For a thousand years, they lived and reigned with Christ.

Here, Father Pansophius wished to end his narrative, which had for its object not a universal cataclysm of creation but the conclusion of our historical process which consists in the appearance, glorification, and destruction of the Anti-Christ.

POLITICIAN – And do you think that this conclusion is so near?

MR. Z. – Well, there will be still some chatter and fuss on the stage, but the whole drama is written to the end, and neither actors nor audience will be permitted to change anything in it.

LADY – But what is the absolute meaning of this drama? I still do not understand why the Anti-Christ hates God so much, while he himself is essentially good, not evil.

MR. Z. – That is the point. He is not *essentially* evil. All the meaning is in that. I take back my previous words that

"You cannot explain the Anti-Christ by proverbs alone."
He can be explained by a simple proverb, "All that glitters
is not gold." You know all too well this glitter of counterfeit
gold. Take it away and no real force remains — none.

GENERAL – But you notice, too, upon what the curtain
falls in this historical drama — upon war — the meeting of
two armies. So our conversation ends where it began. How
does that please you, Prince? Prince? Good heaven! Where's
the Prince?

POLITICIAN – Didn't you notice? He left quietly during
that moving passage where the Elder John presses the
Anti-Christ to the wall. I did not want to interrupt the
reading at that time and, afterward, I forgot.

GENERAL – I bet he ran away — ran away a second time!
He mastered himself the first time and came back, but this
was too much for the poor fellow. He couldn't stand it.
Dear me! Dear me!

THE END

Afterword

SOLOVYOV,
A Prophet for All Seasons
by Stephan A. Hoeller

When we observe many of the outstanding personalities of the past from an historical perspective, we find two categories of persons. The first consists of those individuals who received acclaim in their own times, but whose stature steadily diminished after their death; while the second consists of those who seem, as it were, to be placed ahead of us in time, rather than in the past. The greatness of such figures becomes increasingly clear with the passage of time; their stature is enhanced rather than diminished after their passing through history. Though time has exiled them to the magic land beyond the confines of mortal life, the utterance of their word from the shadows becomes more potent than it ever had been while resounding in the daylight. It might be said that these truly great spirits of humanity loom larger on the screen of time after the passing of the years than in their own lifetimes. Such are considerations that apply to Vladimir Sergeevich Solovyov.

In the wake of World War I and of the Bolshevik revolution, a diaspora of Russian spiritual and intellectual life set in. Still, in these sad and arid years of exile, the message of Solovyov was not absent. In Paris, London, New York, and in other places of refuge, Russian émigré intellectuals turned their attention to the prophetic and mystic legacy of their great countryman. As the seminaries and cathedrals as well as the elegant *salons* of St. Petersburg and Moscow became the ruined playgrounds of Stalin's mob, Solovyov's star rose outside his Russian homeland. Nicholas Berdyayev, Sergei Bulgakov, and a host of scholarly and inspired minds occupied themselves with his works, and his teachings on Sophiology became the mainstay of the famed Institute of St. Sergius in Paris. Many, indeed, are the men and women whose years of exile were rendered bearable, whose weary souls were strengthened, by the spirit of this sage of late nineteenth century Russia.

Meanwhile, in Russia, the believers of the new catacombs and the philosophers of the garrets and the cellars had not forgotten Solovyov either. In 1947, at the height of Stalin's malign power, a religious lay organization with the unassuming name of the Christian Seminar was founded in Moscow. In spite of much persecution, this organization steadily continued to expand its influence and, by the beginning of the 1980's, it was perhaps the most important gathering point for religious intellectuals in the Soviet Union. It had also become the main forum for the study and practice of Solovyov's thought behind the red curtain. By the middle of the same decade, the government sponsored journal *Atheism and Religion* reported the existence of numerous individuals and groups whom it identified as the contemporary reembodiment of the "God-Builders" of prerevolutionary times. The same publication also reported that these religious thinkers were, in the main, disciples of Solovyov. At the same time, far from Russia though close to Solovyov's true spirit, Roman Catholic circles of traditional mystical thought continued to study and elucidate his writings. I can well remember one of my mentors of the 1940's, Alois Wiesinger, a noted expert on the convergences of Hermetic-Occult and Roman Catholic thought, speaking of Solovyov with the greatest admiration. Today, one of France's most influential traditionalist Catholic leaders, the Abbé Georges de Nantes, is also well known as the foremost expert in that country on the work of Vladimir Solovyov.

Solovyov's life has been told elsewhere. Those interested in a detailed biography of considerable contemporary relevance may wish to avail themselves of *Vladimir Soloviev: Russian Mystic* by Paul M. Allen (Blauvelt, New York: Steinerbooks, 1978). Solovyov was born at the beginning of the era during which Russia was to experience its greatest and most painful spiritual conflict — the clash between Western European and homegrown Slavic ideas. Fifty years earlier, the great liberal Tsar, Alexander I, grandson of Catherine the Great, initiated a process of cultural and spiritual alchemy which he intended as the unifier of Western Slavic spiritual currents. Like so many members of the Romanoff dynasty, Alexander was deeply attracted to mystical spirituality and to what might be called the occult. In the course of his extensive travels outside Russia — he was the chief conqueror of Napoleonic France and was lionized in all the capitals of Europe — the young and brilliant ruler came into contact with many mysterious streams of alternative spirituality. The latter part of the eighteenth and the beginning of the nineteenth century throughout Europe were characterized by a considerable resurgence of heterodox ideas and movements. In France, the former Abbé, and later esotericist, Bernard Fabre-Palaprat revived the suppressed Knights Templar under Gnostic auspices. In Germany, the brilliant esotericist, Franz von Baader, addressed himself to the rehabilitation and the Kabbalistic and alchemical mysticism of Jacob Boehme. The courts of kings and princes, too, were teeming with magicians, astrologers, and Masonic adepts. Guided by the seership of his soothsayer, Baroness Krudener, Tsar

Alexander tried to weld Slavic mysticism and Western hermeticism into an abiding unity on Russian soil, even as he forged the Holy Alliance of Christian monarchs in the European arena. Alexander thus began a process that deeply affected many outstanding Russian thinkers, a process which is still not without its effects today.

Although Alexander's successor, Tsar Nicholas I, inclined toward a withdrawal from Western influences, the alchemical *opus* initiated by Alexander continued. The complementary opposites of Russian Orthodox Christianity and European heterodox mysticism never ceased to struggle, embrace, and combine in literature, art, philosophy, and education. There can be little doubt that one of the living vessels of this *opus* was Vladimir Solovyov. The year of his birth, 1853, fell in the era of the disastrous Crimean War, which was instrumental in turning Nicholas I implacably against the West. Intellectuals with westernizing sympathies were censured: Dostoevski, already famous for his work, *Poor Folk*, was exiled to Siberia; Turgenev was in enforced exile on his mother's estate. Gogol, the great novelist, was dead, and the restless, brooding Count Tolstoy had left St. Petersburg in disgust and was serving with a regiment of Cossack cavalry in Southern Russia. It was not a good time for those who looked to horizons outside of Holy Russia for spiritual sustenance. But history, and Vladimir Solovyov were to change all that.

Most thinkers of any historical era organize their experience around ideas. One might say that in these cases life imitates thought. Solovyov does not fit this model. Neither ideas, nor philosophical speculations, nor even theological dogmas were the foundation of Solovyov's life but, rather, a number of mystical experiences which began early in life and continued intermittently until his death. Attending Ascension Day service while still a young boy, he saw the walls and dome of the church disappear and their place taken by a radiant female figure holding a heavenly flower in her hand. Deeply affected, Solovyov discussed his vision with his grandfather, a priest in the Orthodox church. Together, they reached the conclusion that the celestial visitor was Sophia, the Lady of Divine Wisdom, who is recognized by the Orthodox church as a *hypostasis* or emanation of God. The mysterious vision of this Lady, whom he named his "Eternal Friend," returned to Solovyov on several occasions. The next time was when he was studying in England. He called upon her for guidance and she directed him to proceed to Egypt where he might meet her. Spending the night among the Pyramids in solitary vigil, Solovyov at last glimpsed the mystic vision of Sophia in all its transcendental splendor. Before he fell into a trancelike swoon of utter ecstasy, he made her a promise: "Ever will your heavenly roses bloom within me, wherever my stream of life may flow."

Back in Russia, Solovyov labored relentlessly for causes which he believed were dear to his Eternal Friend. Among these was the prospect of the reunification of the Russian Orthodox and Roman Catholic churches. Needless to say, this idea was not received with much sympathy by the Orthodox clergy who generally despised all things Western, including the Roman Catholic form of Christianity. Solovyov, however, had visited Rome and was convinced of the virtue and authenticity of the Papacy. Thus he betook himself to a representative of the Church of Rome and on February 18, 1896, first recited the Creed in its Roman Catholic wording and took communion according to the Latin rite. It is still a matter of dispute whether these actions might be interpreted as a formal conversion on his part from Orthodoxy to Roman Catholicism. Viewed from the perspective of nearly a century, it seems more likely that he merely wished to show a certain solidarity with *both* Orthodox and Roman Catholic churches as a symbol of the desired ecumenicity that might lead to the reunion of the two religious bodies and their traditions of Christianity. Death came early to the noble lover of Lady Wisdom. He died in the first year of the twentieth century, at the age of forty-seven. On his lifeless breast were placed two icons: one of the Virgin Mary, and one of the Divine Sophia. It is to be hoped that these two Holy Ladies duly prepared his way to a world greater and more glorious than the one he left. In less than a quarter of a century his unhappy homeland would succumb to the floodtide of a political system that represented so much that was alien to both the Russian soul and the soul of Solovyov. It would be seventy years before that tide began to withdraw from Russian soil!

If we accept, as we must, that Solovyov's work and thought are rooted in his experience of Sophia, it becomes necessary for us to inquire into the nature and origin of this figure. Inquiry reveals that Solovyov's Eternal Friend appears first in such relatively late Biblical writings as *The Book of the Wisdom of Solomon* and *Proverbs*. In these she is presented as a manifestation of God — feminine, divine or quasi-divine, and of exquisite loveliness. To one conversant with the language employed, there can be little doubt that these scriptures speak of Wisdom as a person, and not as a mere romanticized and poeticized quality of consciousness. The same figure, known in Hebrew as *Chokmah*, also appears in the writings of the hellenistic Jewish philosopher, Philo of Alexandria, who likewise treats her as a personified emanation of God. The *lingua franca* of the world of the New Testament was Greek and therefore, in the first centuries of the Christian era, *Chokmah* was translated *Sophia*.

The figure of Sophia did not attain its highest and most complex differentiation until the arising and flowering of the school of thought known to subsequent centuries as "Gnosticism." The gnostics (from the Greek *gnosis* or knowledge) were Christians who were able to regard the teachings brought by Jesus in the light of personal, transcendental experience. Their orientation was both rooted in and aimed at such experience and they had little use for belief that was not closely connected with it. Gnostic Christians were devoted to myth and sacrament; the former being the expression of their experience of the transcendental truths of existence, while the latter were considered by them not only to be the means of grace but also the means of liberation from the fetters of the unconsciousness that is attendant upon earthly life. The gnostics are frequently characterized as people who sought salvation through knowledge instead of through faith, but this definition may be considered inadequate unless it is amended by stating that the salvific knowledge sought by the gnostics must be primarily understood as self-knowledge — which in its turn brings knowledge of God. Gnostics (not unlike Hindus and Buddhists) held that the deepest, most essential core of the human being is of identical nature with God; and that, therefore, self-knowledge of the highest order achieves a unitive conjunction with the Deity. One of the most important Gnostic myths, in which the experience of salvific self-knowledge is expressed, is the myth of Sophia.

The Gnostic Sophia is a divinely emanated being, descending from the primordial pair of highest divinity. Though a daughter of the highest God, she becomes separated from her source and from the balanced transcendental order of which she was a part. Thereby, she enters the realm of imperfection and darkness where she suffers dire indignities. However, throughout her trials she never abandons confidence in the Light of God and in the powers of redemption. For this reason, in several Gnostic scriptures, she is referred to as *Pistis* (faithful) Sophia. Time and again, Sophia calls out for help from the higher powers; and eventually her pleas meet with the required response. Christ, her Heavenly Bridegroom, descends from on high and, after having enlisted the aid of several great angels and other powers of light, he leads her out of the realm of chaotic darkness, finally restoring her to her original place and position among the supernal aeons of light and love. Sophia's liberation does not, however, estrange her from the earth and human beings for, according to some versions of the myth, she remains forever after mystically accessible to those who deserve her attention. Together with her Bridegroom, Christ, she becomes the co-redeemer of all souls, a feminine savior in her own right.

While Roman Catholicism has officially excised all references to Lady Wisdom from its teachings (although in disguised form she is present in the writings of numerous Catholic saints, as well as in the Black Madonnas of iconography), the Greek and other Orthodox churches continue to refer to her in their theology, which possess a branch called "Sophiology" devoted to her. It was this Greek, or rather Byzantine, Christianity that the lands of Russia adopted a little over one thousand years ago when, as Czeslaw Milosz says in his Introduction, the emissaries of Prince Vladimir reported to their sovereign, after they had attended liturgy in the Cathedral of Hagia Sophia, that the Greeks indeed worshipped God in a manner far more *beautiful* than the worship of other peoples. Thus, Russia came to accept Christianity neither on the basis of its abstract truth, nor of its superior morality, but on account of its *beauty* — a memorable choice which, it seems, she has never lived to regret.

Russia thus inherited the mysterious Sophia from the Greeks. But this was not all that she inherited. Byzantine Christianity acted as the funnel through which Gnostic, Manichean, Neoplatonic, and other ancient and often heterodox influences penetrated the lands of Rus. The Neoplatonic mysticism of (Pseudo)Dionysius the Areopagite, the mystical traditions of St. John the Evangelist by way of Irenaeus, the apostolic gnosis through Clement of Alexandria and Origen — all of these and many more entered Holy Russia by way of Byzantium. As early as the classical age of hellenistic Gnosticism, the Syrian gnostic teacher Bardesanes reportedly travelled to Southern Russia, while Manichean and Neomanichean (Bogomil) missionaries infiltrated there from Bulgaria and Greece. Indeed it may be rightly said that at least some circles of Russian Orthodoxy were always more than a little heterodox at heart.

Among such heterodox members of the Russian Orthodox communion we may most assuredly number Vladimir Solovyov. When he applied to the University of Moscow in 1875 for a travelling scholarship to England, he noted in his application that he intended to study Gnostic, Indian, and Medieval philosophies. The order in which he listed his areas of interest is significant, but it is by no means the only evidence of his involvement with Gnostic thought. His numerous poems dealing with the figure of Sophia indicate quite clearly that his Sophia was in many ways one with the Sophia of the Gnostics. He wrote invocations to Sophia that are dilated with Gnostic, Kabbalistic, and Hermetic terminology and metaphors. Perhaps the most remarkable of these poems is the celebrated "Song of the Ophites," which may be regarded as Solovyov's Gnostic act of faith and whose imagery anticipates in a startling manner C.G. Jung's gnostic and visionary treatise *The Seven Sermons to the Dead*. It may be important to note that the Ophites were a particularly controversial gnostic sect who were accused of all sorts of abominations by the Church Fathers of their day. No conventional Christian of any stripe would readily associate himself with the Ophites. That Solovyov sympathetically extols their views in his poem clearly represents an act of courage and independence on his part. Moreover, his works dealing with the nature of Christianity — such as

The Religious Foundations of Life (1884), *The History and Future of Theocracy* (1885–87), and *The Dogmatic Development of the Church* (1886) — bear witness to his strong Gnostic orientation. In these works he clearly states that, beyond all the various stages of religious belief and practice, as well as beyond all intellectual pursuits such as philosophy, there exists a higher stage of religion based upon personal transcendental experience which is, in content, theosophic and theurgic, i.e., magical. The notion that Solovyov was a kind of nineteenth century gnostic is neither novel nor unusual. None other than his spiritual heir, Nicholas Berdyayev identified him as such. It may also be noted that detractors of both Solovyov and Berdyayev frequently refer to both men as Gnostics. At the same time, however, both were and are held in high esteem as lay theologians and philosophers of Russian Orthodoxy. Seldom was the term "orthodox" applied to a more brilliant and more heterodox pair!

It may be a meaningful consideration of some import that the revival of interest in Vladimir Solovyov, both here and in Russia, coincides with a minor Gnostic renaissance, brought about in large measure by the discovery of the Nag Hammadi library of gnostic writings. In December 1945, an Egyptian peasant, digging for fertilizer near the settlement of Nag Hammadi in Upper Egypt, came upon a jar containing a large number of ancient papyrus codices originating in the third century A.D. A complete, one-volume translation of these texts having appeared in English in 1977, interest both in scholarly circles and among the general public has been mounting ever since. Never has there been such a wealth of literature disclosing the true teachings of the Gnostics. While in Solovyov's days, students had to be satisfied with a mere handful of ancient fragments (supplemented by biased and hostile accounts rendered by some Church Fathers) twelve large codices containing fifty-two separate treatises of unquestionable authenticity have now been made available. The process of reinterpreting and assimilating the Gnostic message has thus been dramatically accelerated.

Even more recently, at the outset of the last decade of the twentieth century, dramatic and well-nigh miraculous events have occurred in Solovyov's homeland. According to all indications, the long night of terror and alienation may at last be over, and a new-old light may be dawning in the East. The political changes in Russia hold the promise of radically changing the religious landscape of the land.

Holy Russia is in the process of being reborn. Intact in its ancient liturgy, tempered by the fire of martyrdom, filled with mystic fervor and sweet devotion, the Russian Orthodox church returns now into plain view once more. With the rise of traditional Russian spirituality come great opportunities for the West also. It may come to pass that the long repressed but never corrupted true soul of Russia has treasures to offer to the spirituality of Europe and America. These are sorely needed. Strange encounters beckon; mystic meetings are at hand.

In the title of this Afterword, I have called Solovyov a "Prophet". This title has been popularly applied to those who foretell the future, however it rather and properly describes one who is a friend and instrument of God. Still, we must remember that Solovyov was deeply concerned for the future and that, in it, he saw many dangers but also much opportunity. Nowhere is this prophetic spirit more clearly manifest than in his work *War, Progress, and the End of History: Three Conversations*, to which is appended his chilling parable "A Short Story of the Anti-Christ." Lindisfarne Press (already distinguished by the publication of Solovyov's *The Meaning of Love*) may now be said to multiply already apparent synchronicities by reprinting Solovyov's prophetic conversations about the end of history and the considerations attendant upon it. For there are many today who regard the present era as indeed the end of history; and the notion that our time may not merely be a *fin de siècle* but a *fin de l'âge* is gaining adherents. In such times, it may be particularly useful to explore the impressions and intuitions offered to us by one of the great souls and sincere hearts of recent times. The gentle lover of Lady Wisdom, Vladimir Sergeevich Solovyov asks no more of us than this and, were he with us today, he would assuredly accept no less.

CPSIA information can be obtained at www.ICGtesting.com

232659LV00004B/6/P

9 780940 262355